FUNDAMENTALS
OF
CONDUCTING

by

Frank Noyes

Head, Department of Violin
Drake University
and
Conductor Drake-Des Moines Symphony

WM. C. BROWN COMPANY
Publishers
DUBUQUE, IOWA

Manufactured by WM. C. BROWN CO. INC., Dubuque, Iowa
Printed in U. S. A.

Introduction

The student who aspires to become a conductor must acquire, through study, a skilled baton technique and a thorough knowledge of the theoretical phases of conducting. To facilitate his study this book is divided into two sections--the practical and the theoretical. It is suggested that these two parts be studied simultaneously thus integrating the two aspects of conducting and, thereby, sustaining the student's interest.

This text is designed for a one semester to one year course of study for the beginning conducting student. The content is planned primarily for the orchestral conductor, however, the problems of baton technique and musicianship encountered by the orchestral director are fundamental in any field of conducting.

The graduates of our college and university music schools become the conductors of the thousands of elementary, high school and college orchestras, bands and choruses as well as the many amateur, semi-professional and professional ensembles throughout the country. They must be prepared to be responsible for the standards of performance of these organizations and for the development, in many instances, of an appreciation of music among the countless performers under their direction who may never become professional musicians but who are eventually included in our listening audiences. The influence that these young conductors will have in establishing a high level of musical performance and appreciation is immeasurable. In a sense, then, their future responsibility becomes as great or greater than that of a Toscanini or a Mitropoulos and they must therefore be given the best possible conducting education.

This book endeavors to give the beginning conducting student groundwork he will need as well as many hints which he might learn otherwise only through long and trying experience. It is hoped that thorough study of this text will place the young student a long way on the road to becoming a capable conductor.

Frank Noyes

Des Moines, Iowa

February, 1954

Acknowledgments

The author wishes to gratefully acknowledge the valuable advice and comment given him by: Dr. Gordon Bird, Professor Stanley Hess, Dean Frank B. Jordan, Dr. Francis J. Pyle, Professor Don R. Marcouiller and Professor Stanford Hulshizer of the College of Fine Arts of Drake University; Professor Mildred Jessup of the Liberal Arts College and Professor Hiram S. Hunn of the Community College of Drake University; Associate Professors Frank W. Hill and Roland Searight of Iowa State Teachers College, Thomas Cox of Des Moines, Dick O. Wilson, Director of Music at Des Moines Technical School and Dr. Thor Johnson, Musical Director of the Cincinnati Symphony Orchestra, Cincinnati, Ohio.

The first page of Sevilla by I. Albeniz is used by permission of the Edward B. Marks Music Corporation.

The first page of American Salute by Morton Gould is used by permission of the Mills Music Company, Inc.

The first page and the seventh page of Toccata by Frescobaldi and arranged for orchestra by Hans Kindler is used by permission of the Mills Music Company, Inc.

Table of Contents

(Study Parts I and II simultaneously)

PART I - PRACTICAL ASPECTS

PART II - THEORETICAL ASPECTS

PART I - PRACTICAL ASPECTS

CHAPTER I
Holding the Baton

This chapter is to be devoted to the first steps in actually using the baton. This beginning period, as in the study of an instrument, is a vitally important time in your life as a young conductor. You must use the utmost care to establish the kind of beat discussed in Chapter VII of Part II, namely an authoritative, precise beat and one which is pleasing to watch. Reasonable physical coordination and a willingness to apply yourself assiduously will insure the desired final results.

Your first step must be that of learning to hold a baton. Let us assume that you have your stick and are ready to begin your first lesson in baton technique. Study Figure 1 and note that the thumb and the first two fingers of the hand do the actual holding of the stick.

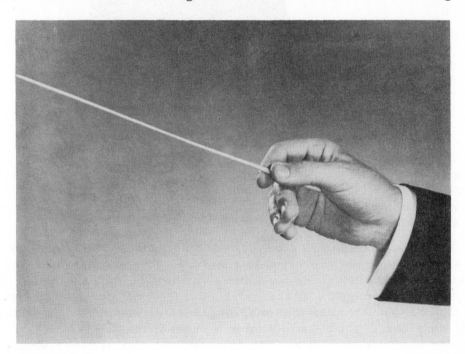

Figure 1

You will also notice that the large end of the baton points toward the center of the palm of the hand and almost touches it. The third and fourth fingers are loose, neither straight nor bent around the baton. Practice picking up the stick many times and try to hold it lightly and yet maintain at the same time a firm control over it.

Study Figure 2 and note that the end of the baton does not point straight away from the body but a little to the left of the straight line formed by the elbow and wrist. This position gives the largest possible number of players a view of more than just the point of the baton. Also observe that the right arm is extended well in front and to the right of the body and that the elbow is slightly bent. The palm of the hand must be parallel with the floor at all

Figure 2

times. These directions are very important, for a fundamental beat pattern must be learned before deviating from it in any way. Notice that the arm and hand slope upward from the elbow gradually and that the wrist breaks slightly. The hand may be parallel with or slightly below a level with the chin which places the baton high enough to be clearly seen by every member of the ensemble.

When the baton feels comfortable in your hand and you are able to grasp it quickly and correctly, you are ready for the exercises in Figure 3. These simple motions are designed as an aid in acquiring flexibility of the hand and arm while holding the baton. Exercises A and B are wide, rapid movements with the wrist only, first up and down in direction and then right and left. C and D are circular motions, clockwise and counter clockwise, using the wrist only. Add the elbow to the wrist action in E thereby making the circles larger. Finally, in F move from the shoulder as well as from the elbow and wrist describing a still larger circle. Use the wrist at all times and move freely in the elbow and shoulder joints. While practicing these exercises keep the left arm at your side.

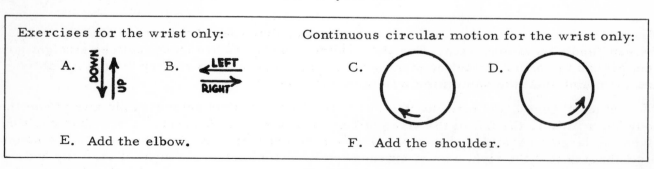

Figure 3

2

Much confidence can be gained by standing on a podium with a music stand in front of you when conducting beat diagrams for the instructor's criticism in a class room situation. A podium should be from six to ten inches in height and about a yard square. The height depends on the conductor's size. It need not be as high for the tall person as for one of shorter stature. The bottom of the beat must not be hidden at any time and the players should not have to look up in an uncomfortable manner to see the top of the beat. The width of the podium must be sufficient to avoid any feeling of insecurity in regard to stepping off the edge.

The music stand should be one of several heavy, adjustable types. It should be set at a height which enables you to turn the pages of the score easily and without having to reach or stoop to do so. However, it should be low enough to avoid the danger of hooking the stand top or score with the baton. More than one conductor has lost his baton in the ensemble before him or in the audience behind him because his music rack was not adjusted at the proper height. Stand firmly and do not walk about. Feel balanced, as you will if your feet are properly spaced. You will note that if you spread your feet too far apart you will immediately feel awkward and if too close you will tend to lose your balance. There is no precise rule to follow in regard to the exact distance apart your feet should be spaced. The important point is that you must feel comfortable, balanced and, above all, relaxed. Relaxation applies to every step in learning to use the arms and hands. This admonition is of vital importance and cannot be overemphasized. The entire body moves freely and smoothly like a well-oiled machine.

THE PREPARATORY BEAT

The preparatory beat consists of two types which may be designated as "silent" or "played". In either case this beat accomplishes three things:

(1) It establishes the tempo of the composition about to be played.
(2) It conveys to the players the general style and dynamic level of the first bars of the composition.
(3) It brings about a simultaneous "attack" or beginning by the group under direction.

Possibly the preparatory motion is the most difficult beat the conductor has to master. Certainly it takes much practice to execute it successfully.

The "silent" preparatory beat is used when the composition being conducted starts on the first beat of the measure without any portion of a measure preceding the first complete bar. See Figure 4.

The beat diagrams in this book are actual pictures taken on film by means of a lighted baton. It should be remembered, in using these photographs for study purposes, that they are, of necessity, detailed as well as a study of the baton patterns of one person. Individual variation is present in the comparison of any two beat technics. It is not suggested that the student must copy every minor detail of these diagrams but, rather, that he use them to obtain the general direction, flexibility and style inherent in a precise and, at the same time, graceful baton technique. Accompanying some

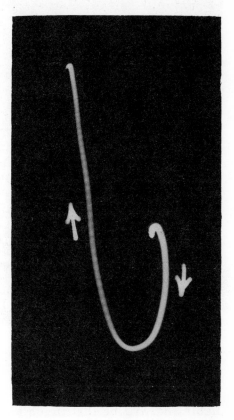

Figure 4. The Preparatory Beat.

3

of the pictures is a simple diagram of the photographed beat pattern. Do not follow these literally but use them as a directional aid only.

Let us discuss the execution of the "silent" preparatory beat at this time, reserving the study of the "played" preparatory beat until the baton technique has been further developed as it is a more complicated motion and requires a knowledge of sub-division before it can be properly studied.

The preparatory beat starts from the arm position already described in this chapter and illustrated on page three. From this position the beat moves down in direction, curves to the left and up for the main body of the movement. It will be observed that the entire pattern resembles somewhat the shape of a fishhook. (Figure 4) The wrist must be very flexible throughout the execution of this beat. However, in a forte, forceful work it moves much less than in a legato, quiet composition. The distance the arm travels depends on the speed and dynamic indications of the music being conducted. The faster the tempo of the work being played the smaller the motion needed. In piano and pianissimo the amount of movement is less than in forte and fortissimo. As the preparatory beat sets the initial tempo for the composition being directed it <u>must be exactly in the speed of the beats to follow</u> regardless of considerations of style and dynamic level.

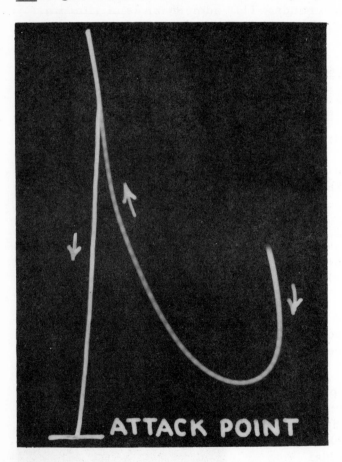

Figure 5. The Attack Point.

Examine Figure 5 carefully before actually attempting preparatory beats. Note where the "attack" takes place. There are at least two great conductors who believe in training their orchestras to wait a moment after the baton has reached this position before making the attack. One of these conductors explains that he obtains a different style of attack because of this hesitation and uses it only in certain instances. Some of the men in that orchestra, however, assert that they are often confused by it and that they must guess as to when the entrance should occur. This type of beat cannot be recommended to young conductors and there is reason to question its success when used by the finest directors.

Practice preparatory beats by having several persons watch you and say the word "play" as they see the attack point. If the word is spoken in unison you probably have a clear and precise motion. <u>The preparatory beat must be the preliminary motion in practicing all beat figures henceforth.</u> Form the habit of placing the arm in preparatory beat position and holding it so for a few seconds before starting the beat. Later, when conducting live groups you will have established this habit and will be that much surer of having the attention of your ensemble and of, thereby, obtaining a clean, precise attack. It is surprising how many student conductors do not follow this simple procedure.

THE TWO BEAT MEASURE

The two-in-a-bar beat is the first complete beat to be studied. Examine Figure 6 and note the movement to the right and up as beat one is completed. The execution of this motion in fast tempo is accomplished by means of the wrist and hand alone. It is a rebound from 1 as indicated by the dotted line in Figure 6. In slower tempo the wrist action to the right will be broader and will include some arm movement. The length of the vertical line as well as the width of this "hooking" motion to the side and upward will always depend upon the time allowed for the beat by the tempo of the composition being conducted as well as by its general style. The second count is in reverse to whatever has been done in executing the first beat. It retraces, in other words, the pattern of the downward motion. Examine Figure 7 for a comparison of this beat in rapid and slow tempo.

Note: (It is suggested that the student confine his practice during the first three chapters of this book to the learning of the beat patterns diagrammed without recourse to the use of musical illustrations of any kind except for visual examination as study progresses. On completion of Chapter III he is ready to select and conduct, as a class assignment, hymns and folk songs or more difficult compositions if his ability warrants it. Each student should direct these compositions in class for criticism by the instructor with a capable pianist at the piano. It is important that the pianist follow the conductor exactly even though mistakes such as poor attacks, faulty tempos, lack of dynamic indications and indistinct cut-offs are made by the student. In other words, the conductor must be made to lead and not follow the instrumentalist.)

Practice this beat, as well as all succeeding ones to be studied, before a mirror. It will be helpful to count aloud during the initial practice of all beat figures, at the same time

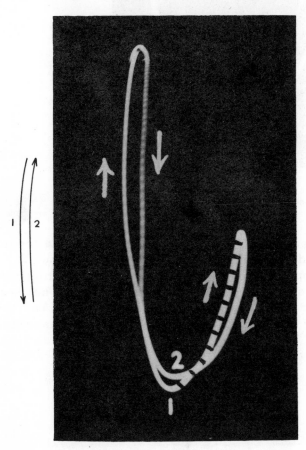

Figure 6. The Two Beat.

Figure 7. Fast and Slow Two Beat.

following the diagram of the measure being studied. Start at a slow tempo, gradually increasing the speed. The right hand is always used to set and keep the tempo while the left hand eventually may hang at one's side or be employed in a variety of ways. The complete function of the left hand will be discussed in detail in Chapter V. For the present the left hand should be used in conjunction with the right hand in describing all beat figures. It must imitate exactly the movements of the right hand. For example, in a two beat figure the left hand moves to the left and up at 2 (see Figure 8) as the right hand moves to the right and up.

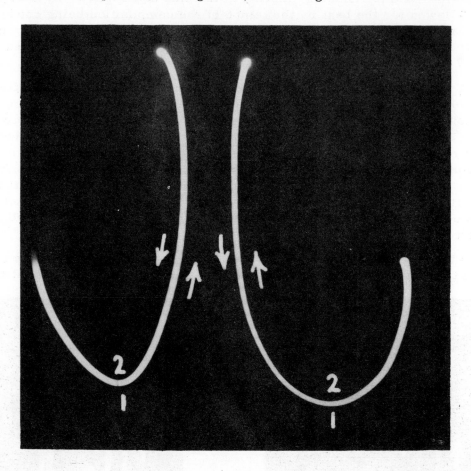

Figure 8. Both Hands in Two.

There are two general types of beat--the legato beat and the staccato beat. The legato motion does not come to a pause between beats while the staccato beat does. The type of beat employed by the conductor depends entirely upon the character of the music. Practice both legato and staccato using the two beat figure shown in Figure 7. Remember the necessity for a flexible wrist in doing either staccato or legato as well as the need for full bodily coordination. Figure 9 gives musical examples of both staccato and legato in two measure.

HUNGARIAN DANCE NO. 1

Allegro molto

Brahms

OVERTURE TO NUTCRACKER SUITE

Allegro giusto

Tchaikovsky

Figure 9

CHAPTER II
The Three Beat Measure

The preparatory beat technique employed in moving to the attack point at number 1 is the same for the three beat measure as for the two beat figure. The difference is in the rebound motion which in three is directly up from 1, veering very slightly to the right as the top of the motion is reached. It is executed, mainly, by means of a snap of the wrist plus a rolling motion of the elbow. The rebound absorbs the shock of the first beat at 1 as well as making possible a more graceful connection between the first and second counts. It varies somewhat in sharpness and width depending on the tempo and style of the composition being conducted but is never omitted entirely. Examine Figure 10 for a diagram of the three measures in slow legato and Figure 11 for the same figure in fast staccato.

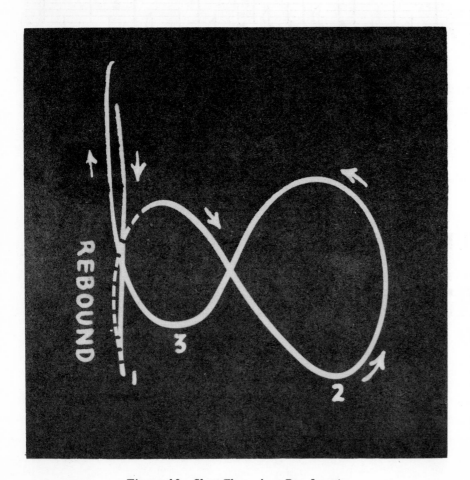

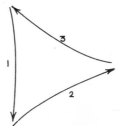

Figure 10. Slow Three in a Bar Legato.

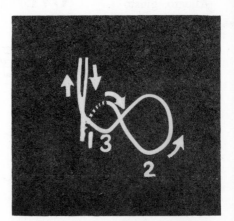

Figure 11. Fast Three in a Bar Staccato.

Move from the top of the rebound to the right and downward slightly to the count of two. Note in Figure 10 that this motion is in the form of a graceful curve rather than a straight line. The degree of curve, again, depends upon the tempo and the style of the music being conducted. In rapid tempo or staccato the curves are, necessarily, somewhat smaller than in legato. The second beat starts at number 2 on the diagram in Figure 10. It is a graceful loop upward, over and down to the lower part of the imaginary vertical line made by the first beat. The third beat starts at number 3 in the diagram and moves immediately upward. Figures 13 and 14 are musical examples of the three measure in slow legato and rapid staccato.

A slight snap of the wrist at all numbered points after 1 in the following diagrams (with the exception of the one in a bar measure which is explained in detail later) will punctuate the beginning of these counts and make the reading of the conductor's beat patterns easier. The result will be better precision of ensemble. These motions must be made within the main flow of the beats and without interrupting them. In three, therefore, this emphasis with the wrist will come at points 2 and 3 on the diagram as given on page 8, Figure 10.

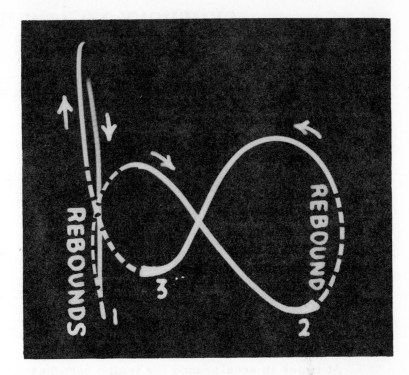

Figure 12

The immediate movement following the numbered points on each beat diagram may be considered a rebound as is that after beat one. However, these rebounds usually are not as pronounced in change of direction as those after the latter. For example, Figure 12 shows the approach to beats 2 and 3 (broadened lines) and the portions which may be considered rebounds (broken lines) as they occur in three measure. The same principle applies in studying all future beat diagrams.

The left hand should be included in practicing the three beat as soon as the right hand can do three comfortably and confidently. It traces the figure described by the right hand exactly which means, of course, that the hands, on the count of two, are at opposite sides of the body. Conduct a full first bar in practicing Figure 14 until the "played" preparatory beat has been studied.

Figure 13

9

SYMPHONY NO. 40, G MINOR, (K.550)

Allegretto — Movement III — Mozart

Figure 14

At times in accelerando the tempo becomes too rapid for three intelligible beats. It is then necessary to do the three measure in what is known as one in a bar. This pattern is a contraction of three into one. It consists in very rapid tempo of a short, fast downward stroke on the count of one, a rebound to the starting point on the count of two and a very slight wait during the count of three before repeating the beat. In other words, the rebound is straight up, but unlike that in other beat patterns it returns all the way to the starting point in one rapid motion. As the tempo is fast before one in a bar need be employed, the distance the hand and arm travel in either direction is quite short. It should be noted that in a slow one in a bar the motion of the hand and arm is one continuous movement with no pause at the count of three unless the style is marcato or staccato in which case there must be a slight pause. In either form of this beat pattern a flexible wrist is most important. Examine Figure 15 for a picture comparing this beat in slow and rapid tempo. The counts of 2 and 3 are placed in this figure to assist the student in understanding the difference in the technique in describing the fast and slow one in a bar. These counts are automatically included in the motion of 1 and its rebound and they are not actually marked by the baton.

Figure 16 is a musical example of a slow one in a bar while Figure 17 is the same in rapid tempo.

Figure 18 is conducted in a moderate one for the first twelve bars, changing suddenly to a three beat at the beginning of measure thirteen and returning to one at the a tempo mark. In practicing the change from three beats to one in a bar count at a moderate speed gradually increasing the tempo. Just before the beat becomes too rapid to be intelligible in three change to one in a bar. It is important that this measure be practiced both in three and in one at varying speeds and that the student drill on the change without pause

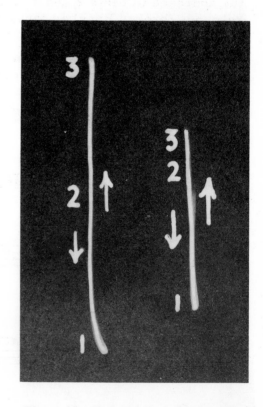

Figure 15. Slow and Fast One in a Bar.

10

FANDANGO ASTURIANO from
CAPRICCIO ESPAGNOL

Rimsky-Korsakow

Figure 16

SYMPHONY NO. 6, F MAJOR, Op. 68
(Pastoral)
Movement III

Beethoven

Figure 17

TALES FROM THE VIENNA WOODS

Tempo di Waltz

Strauss

Figure 18

11

from three to one and return, again, to three. Do this by imagining a certain definite number of bars of accelerando in three, a like number in one and then a return to three by making a gradual ritard to the original tempo.

THE FOUR BEAT MEASURE

Several points should be noted carefully and incorporated into the four beat technique. The first beat and rebound are done as in three with the exception that the rebound tends to move slightly to the left in this pattern rather than to the right as it does in the three figure. At the top of the first beat rebound the movement is to the left and downward in a graceful curve. Count 1 ends and count 2 starts (at number 2 on Figure 19) with an upward motion of the hand and arm covering a distance of from four to eight inches, depending on the speed and style of beat being employed. At the top of this upward movement the hand completes a graceful loop moving now to the right and downward slightly. The hand crosses an imaginary vertical line in front of the conductor and continues to a position as far to the right for beat 3 as it has been to the left at the beginning of beat 2. From this point another loop and downward motion places the hand in position for the 4 count which is actually a preparatory beat in execution. In four, as in three, the amount of curve employed in any one beat depends upon the speed and character of the music. There is danger of too much rather than too little curve, however, resulting in a "pretzel" pattern which is difficult to follow. When using both hands do not allow them to cross each other at the moment the second beat is completed. Consult Figure 19 for the four measure diagram and Figure 20 for a musical example. Emphasize beats 2, 3 and 4 with a snap of the wrist in practicing the four beat as was described on pages 8 and 9 for the three measure. Conduct a complete first bar in Figure 20 for the present.

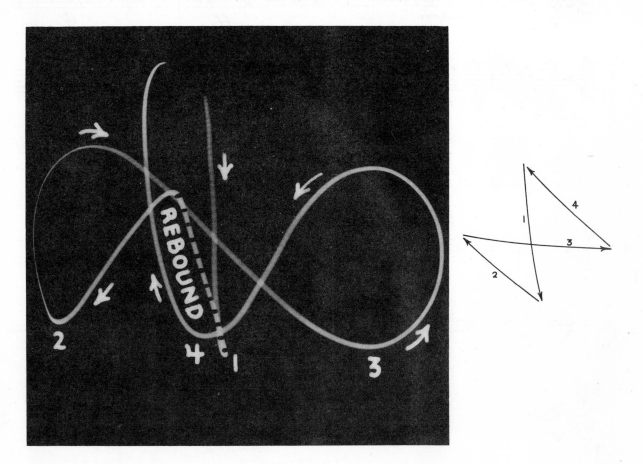

Figure 19

SYMPHONY NO. 6, B MINOR, Op. 74

(Pathetique)
Movement I

Andante   Tchaikovsky

Figure 20

THE SIX BEAT MEASURE

The most commonly used pattern in six is diagrammed in Figure 21 and is the best one of several for the student to learn. The rebound is the same as in the three beat bar.

The second beat starts at Figure 2 in the diagram and is a short curved line like this: . It is executed with a combination of wrist and arm movement. The third beat is a graceful loop upward in direction, over and down which leads into the beginning of the fourth count at numeral 4. It is a broad stroke from left to right across the imaginary vertical line described by the down beat. As the six beat measure is almost always divided rhythmically

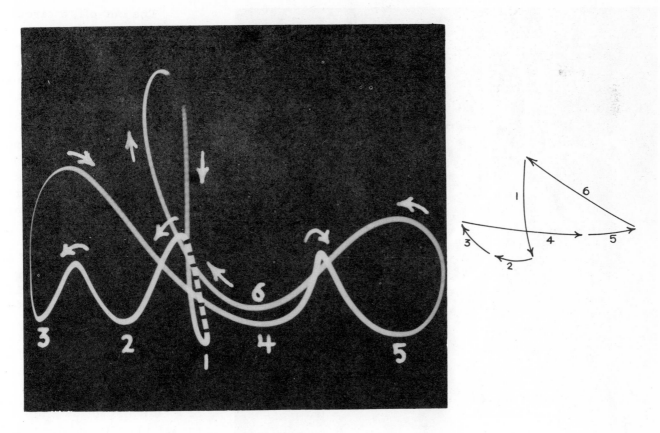

Figure 21. The Six Beat.

PRELUDE TO TRISTAN AND ISOLDE

Figure 22

into two equal parts, this broader third count marks firmly the end of the first half of the measure and for that reason is an aid to the eyes of the players concerned. It is, of course, not a slower beat than the others in elapsed time but simply covers more distance. Some

students tend to make 2, 3, 4, and 5 over rather than under in direction like this:  .
The pattern as diagrammed ⌣⌣ in Figure 21 is much to be preferred. Six beat bars may be reduced to two beats when the tempo is too fast for an efficient six. When this occurs the two beat bar, already diagrammed in Figure 6, is used. See Figure 22 for musical example in six.

THE CUT-OFF

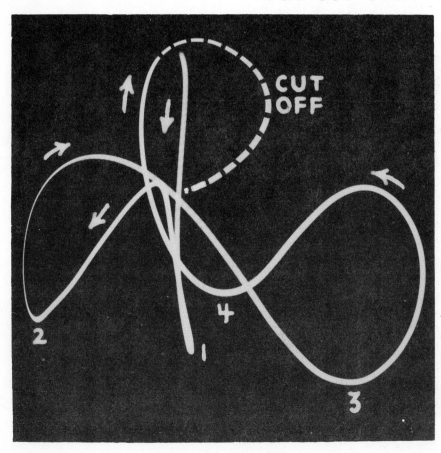

Figure 23. The Cut-Off.

The cut-off, a circular motion to the right, downward and to the left, stops the ensemble and is a signal which must be given precisely and timed accurately if a clean release is to be achieved. Figure 23 shows the cut-off as executed on the last beat of four at a slow or moderately fast speed. Note the preparatory motion upward and to the right (dotted line) before the downward movement takes place. Figure 24 is a picture of the cut-off on the second count of three. The cut-off motion may be made to the left in direction as in this instance, if this seems more natural or places the baton in a better position to continue to the next beat.

The release at the end of a composition is almost invariably a broad downward sweep of the hands so that the conductor may drop his arms to his side at the completion of the cut-off with the minimum of movement. (Figure 25). An exception to this rule, however, is sometimes seen in the technique employed in conducting a pianissimo last bar when the music fades away to a whisper. In such instances the hands, remaining high, may very quietly and slowly describe the cut-off figure. The cut-off is completed as the hands pause on finishing the circular movement. After the release has been made the hands remain where they are for a moment before dropping them to the respective sides of the body.

When the last bar of a composition consists of a full chord with no moving parts it is permissible, if desired, to stop beating. In such cases the hands are held high and are not moved until the cut-off signal is started. If this technique is used in conducting a final bar it is wise to count the necessary beats mentally to be certain that the wait before signaling the release is one full bar. For instance, if the last bar ends with a whole note in four-four

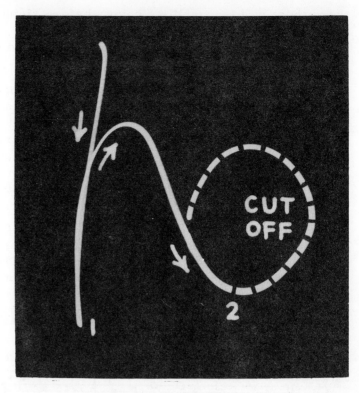

Figure 24. The Cut-Off.

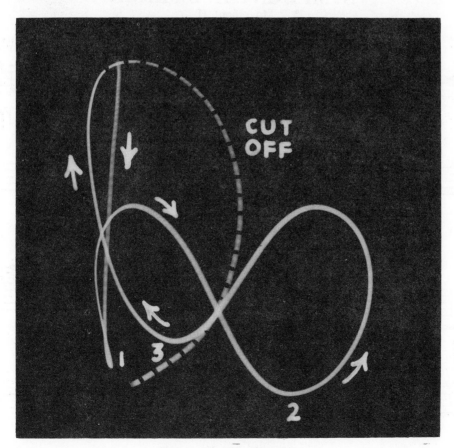

Figure 25. The Cut-Off.

there must be four complete counts before signaling for the cut-off. It may help to add an
imaginary note making the release on the added note as follows:

When temporary cessation of the music occurs during the course of a composition the cut-off is indicated by the circular motion already described. The size of this motion will depend upon the vigor and speed of the music at that point. It is vitally important, however, to finish the release motion so that the hands are in position to go on immediately and without awkwardness in the direction of the next beat following the pause. For this reason be careful never to allow the hands to drop too low in such cut-offs. Very often the left hand indicates a cut-off to part of the ensemble while the right hand continues the beat for the remaining players who continue without pause.

There are three examples in Figure 26 of the use of the cut-off during the course of a composition. The hands remain high in these examples as the cut-off is completed in order to be in position to continue to the next beat. The circular motion to the right or left is employed regardless of the beat upon which the cut-off occurs although the motion may be small and rapid.

Figure 26

16

CHAPTER III
Variance of the Beat

Variance of the beat occurs when the steady flow of the right hand is interrupted in describing any one of the various regular beat patterns. These variations are found mainly in sub-division, "played" preparatory beats, holds, accelerandos, ritards and recitatives. Let us examine the technique employed in conducting each of these beat variations:

SUB-DIVISION

Sub-division is employed in very slow tempo when the speed of the composition being directed is too slow for the conventional beat to be easily followed by the players. It is especially needed when more than one note is written to a beat unit. The first bars of the SYMPHONY NO. 92 in G MAJOR (OXFORD) by Haydn are an example of a work in three-four which should be conducted in a sub-divided beat (Figure 27). Figure 28 is a diagram of three measure sub-divided.

SYMPHONY NO. 92, G MAJOR
(Oxford)
Movement II

Adagio   Haydn

Figure 27

17

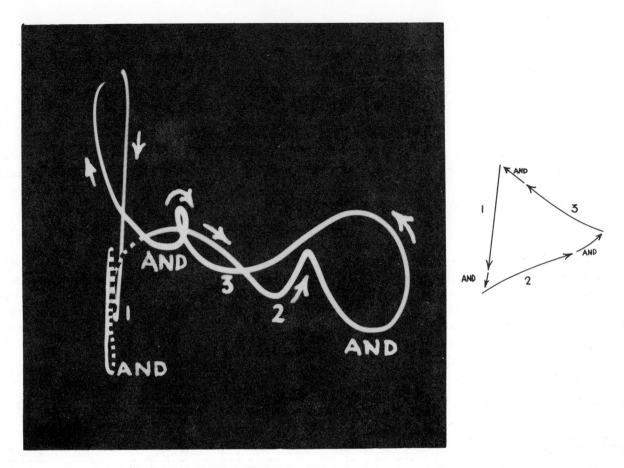

Figure 28. Subdivided Three.

These introductory bars are written in three-four but are conducted in six--a sub-divided three. If this passage were to be directed in three the length of each beat would make the precise execution of the eighth notes difficult. In a sub-divided three the problems of ensemble are greatly simplified. Note that Figure 28 is not a six beat figure but is a sub-divided three. The need of sub-division corresponds somewhat to the need of a gear shift on a bicycle in ascending a steep hill.

Figure 29 is an excerpt from a TOCCATA by Frescobaldi--arranged by Kindler-- which is conducted in a sub-divided four beat. Figure 30 is this beat diagrammed.

There are two things to keep in mind in executing sub-division:

(1) Be certain that the tempo is not disturbed in changing the main beat pattern to a sub-divided one. Practice changing to subdivision during ritards.

(2) Emphasize slightly the first or main beat of the sub-divided group and keep the succeeding beats in each unit smaller and moving in the same direction as that of the main beat. Practice the sub-division examples in Figure 31.

"PLAYED" PREPARATORY BEAT

The "played" preparatory beat consists of any part of a measure preceding the first complete bar at the beginning of a composition. The same situation may occur following a definite pause during the course of a work. The problem for the conductor in such instances, whether consisting of one note or several, is that of giving a clear, preparatory motion.

18

TOCCATA

Frescobaldi-Kindler

Figure 29

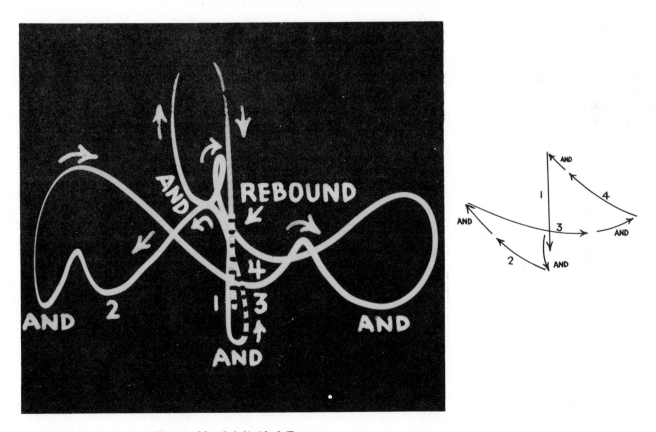

Figure 30. Subdivided Four.

Figure 31.

There are two basic ways to conduct the "played" preparatory beat:

(1) If the attack comes at the beginning of a complete count conduct one full silent preparatory beat. This beat must not be large enough to cause a false entrance (wrist action, alone, is usually sufficient) and the baton must move in the direction it would normally take in the beat pattern being employed. Examine Figure 32 for a musical problem of this kind.

(2) If the attack falls on any fraction of a full count conduct only the beat on which the entrance occurs. Study Figure 33 for musical examples. The first excerpt from the Sibelius symphony No. 2, D major, Op. 43, is conducted in two. The second example under Figure 33 from Haydn's SYMPHONY NO. 100, G MAJOR (MILITARY) is conducted in two and is an example of the preparatory beat problem as it occurs on a fraction of a full count when that beat has already been indicated. The technique here requires the repetition of the second count of measure two following the hold, cut-off and slight pause for the long eighth rest.

All rules have exceptions. There are at least two cases when this latter technique described under (2) may fail:

(A) The players must have time to gauge the tempo, breathe or put their bows into motion. A preparatory beat given in rapid tempo may not make this possible, thereby causing less than a crisp, unified attack. On occasion the solution is the use of a small, silent preparatory beat, in the tempo of the composition, before the attack beat. Figure 34 is a musical example which might in execution include a short, silent beat to the right preceding the attack beat.

(B) The same technique may be employed when there is a single short note preceding the first full bar. This is especially difficult from the ensemble standpoint when written for full orchestra. (Figure 35) It must be emphasized that the added silent preparatory beat should be employed only when there is reason to

NOCTURNE FROM MIDSUMMER NIGHT'S DREAM

Andante tranquillo

Mendelssohn

CLASSICAL SYMPHONY, D MAJOR, Op. 25

Allegro non troppo · Movement III · Prokofieff

Figure 32

SYMPHONY NO. 2, D MAJOR, Op. 43

Allegretto · Movement I · Sibelius

SYMPHONY NO. 100, G MAJOR
(Military)

Presto · Movement IV · Haydn

Figure 33

OBERON

Allegro con fuoco · Weber

Figure 34

Andante maestoso

BARBER OF SEVILLE

Rossini

Figure 35

be concerned in regard to the securing of a unified and precise attack as might be the case if one were conducting an inexperienced ensemble or one which needed this assistance while learning a composition. Many professional conductors use this method of securing a unified attack. It is not to be considered amateurish. Serge Koussevitzky gave three complete bars before the attack bar in conducting the Scherzo of the Beethoven Symphony No. 5, C Minor, Op. 67 in order to establish the tempo and be certain of a precise entrance by the bass viols and cellos. (Figure 36) Certain it is that an ensemble appreciates this added assistance in making an entrance, especially the wind players.

SYMPHONY NO. 5, C MINOR, Op. 67

Movement III

Allegro

Beethoven

Figure 36

Many players are grateful to the conductor who gives a silent beat in such instances as described under (A) and (B). This technique in conducting the "played" preparatory beat, coming on a fraction of the count, is especially helpful in directing amateur and school orchestras which do not include many strong players in their personnel. It is equally helpful in conducting the professional orchestra when unfamiliar works are being read. The conductor should not hesitate to use the added silent beat as preparation for the attack beat when he feels it will clarify this problem.

It may be necessary, occasionally, to experiment with particularly difficult preparatory beat situations, explaining one's technique, demonstrating and rehearsing until a perfect attack is achieved. Execution of the "played" preparatory beat requires considerable judgment on the part of the conductor for he must plan his baton technique so that every player has a clear understanding of exactly when the entrance takes place. Student conductors must practice preparatory beat examples until they are thoroughly at home executing them. Figure 37 shows several additional examples for study purposes.

Figure 37

The words hold, pause and fermata are synonymous and indicate a temporary cessation of the time of the movement, expressed by the sign ⌢ placed over a note or a rest. If over a note the sign signifies that the note is to be prolonged at the pleasure of the conductor; if over a rest, time, as well as the sound, must stop.

Holds, when over a note, may be classified in two general groups--those which are cut-off and those which continue without pause to the next note of the composition. The conductor must determine whether the composer wanted a pause or not, unless the latter has indicated, by rests following the hold or by the signs // or ⸲ , that he definitely wishes a break in the forward progress of the music.

The baton comes to a pause on reaching the cut-off type hold and the release is made with a circular motion, to the left or right, described in Chapter II, Part I, as follows: ☾ ☽ The important thing to note is what follows this type of hold for the hand <u>must</u> be in position to execute the next beat. The left hand may be included, if desired, in making the hold. When used it follows exactly the movement of the right hand. The speed and character of the release motion depends upon the style and speed of the music involved. The faster the tempo, the sharper and smaller the motion of the wrist and the less the arm is employed.

Figure 38 shows examples of the cut-off hold.

SYMPHONY NO. 4, C MINOR
(Tragic)
Movement I

Adagio molto
Schubert

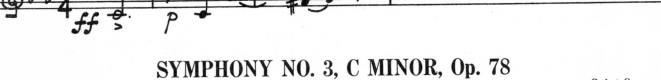

SYMPHONY NO. 3, C MINOR, Op. 78
Movement I

Adagio
Saint-Saens

Figure 38

There are innumerable hold, cut-off combinations possible but all employ the same principle of beat pause followed by the release, with the hands always in position to continue in the direction of the next beat without awkwardness. Occasionally the left hand indicates a hold for part of an ensemble while the right hand continues the beat pattern for the benefit of those players who have a moving part through some or all of the hold. See Figure 39 for examples of these problems. In each of these examples indicate a full count immediately following the cut-off in order to provide ample warning for the attack.

The moving type of hold is comparatively easy, for the conductor does not stop the baton but keeps it in motion through the hold wherever it occurs in the bar. The speed of the baton motion must be gauged entirely by the length of the hold. The movement signifying the hold should be steady and must end with the arm in position to make the next beat.

SYMPHONY NO. 4, D MINOR, Op. 120

Allegro   Movement I   Schumann

TOCCATA

Allegro giusto   Frescobaldi-Kindler

Figure 39

(Figure 40) Indicate this first beat after the hold very firmly and clearly so that there is no question as to the precise moment the hold is terminated. When the hold is over a note of more than one beat in value conduct normally until reaching the last count. Lengthen this final beat the desired amount of time for completion of the hold. (Figures 41 and 42.)

Figure 43 contains an example of the moving hold which is concluded on a portion of the beat in which it occurs. In this instance the second count is repeated. The technique consists of a long second beat to the right indicating the hold followed, in the same direction, by the extra count which signals the end of the hold and the moment for the playing of the sixty-fourth notes.

SYMPHONY NO. 4, B♭ MAJOR; Op. 60

Allegro   Movement IV   Beethoven

Figure 40

25

SUITE IN E MAJOR

Foote

Figure 41

ON HEARING THE FIRST
CUCKOO IN SPRING

Delius

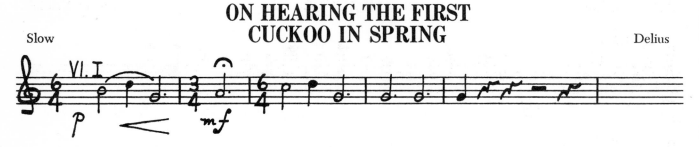

Figure 42

Andante

Mozart

Figure 43

ACCELERANDOS

Accelerate means to move faster or hasten. In conducting this means a gradual increase in the speed of the beat whatever the dynamic marking may be. The timing of an accelerando must be carefully gauged, especially if it is of several bars' duration combined with a crescendo or if a definite new tempo must be established on its completion. Guard against making too much of an increase in speed or making the acceleration too abruptly. When the accelerando continues to a point where, for the sake of clarity, the number of beats in the bar must be reduced (three to one or six to two, for example) the moment chosen for the change must be carefully selected and the baton movement very precise. Improvise examples of such contractions and practice them until they are easily and gracefully done. Figure 44 shows an accelerando combined with a crescendo.

RITARDS

Ritard means to move gradually slower. In a ritard the beat becomes slower and may, at the same time, become broader if the music is vigorous in style. The beat will also become broader if the ritard is coupled with a crescendo or narrower if accompanied by a diminuendo. Ritards must be done smoothly and gradually. The exact amount of tempo change is a matter of musical judgment which must be left to the conductor. Exaggerated effects in a conductor's interpretations are always to be avoided. Such treatment of a

Andante maestoso

LES PRELUDES

Liszt

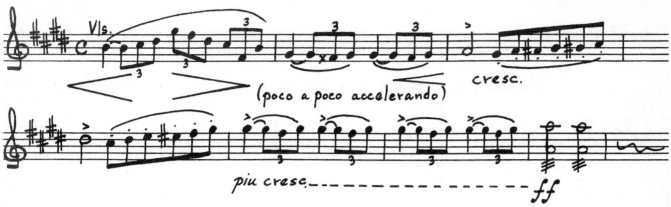

Figure 44

composer's score may be likened to food which has been highly over-seasoned. The cook may be happy about it but no-one else is.

Practice accelerandos and ritards over a definite number of bars and combine them with crescendo and diminuendo, forte and piano. For an example of the diminuendo-ritard see Figure 45.

SYMPHONY NO. 5, E MINOR, Op. 95

(From the New World)

Movement II

Largo

Dvorák

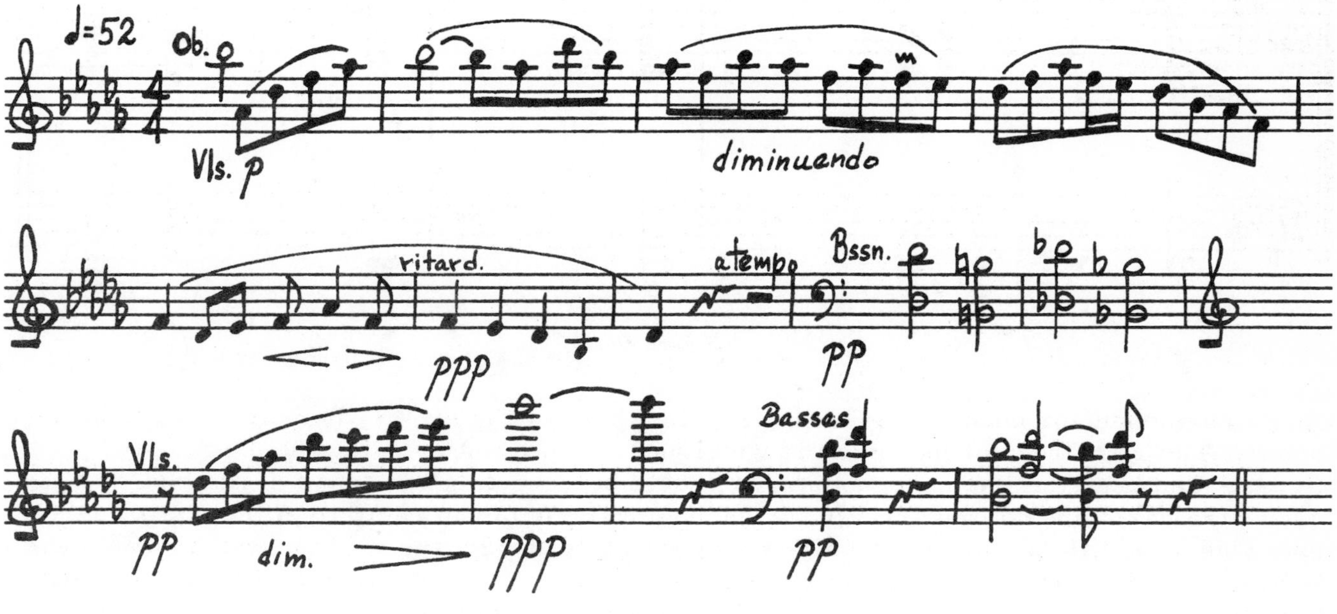

Figure 45

RECITATIVES

Recitative is the name given to the declamatory portions of an opera, oratorio or cantata as opposed to the lyrical. The recitative is accompanied by occasional chords which may be short or sustained. In Figures 46 and 47 both types are seen.

MESSIAH

Handel

Figure 46

The conductor needs to give a broad, firm beat in Figure 46 where the chord changes occur. The remainder of the time the vocal part is followed by using the usual four beat figure. The beats between chord changes should be very small because of the fact that the orchestra parts are not moving. In the second example of the recitative, the short quarter note chords are firmly and precisely conducted while, again, the rests between chords are indicated by very small beats as the conductor follows the solo. In both of these recitatives the two last chords are traditionally played after the completion of the solo. Some conductors prefer to indicate with the baton only the places in the score where chords in the accompaniment occur. This technique is possible with a thoroughly routined orchestra.

The young conductor often feels that, with the mastery of the foregoing beat patterns and their variations, his baton technique is complete. Actually, if he is not to be just a time beater, he must strive at all times to portray with his hands, arms, body and facial expressions the style and mood of the compositions he conducts. It is necessary that he, first,

MESSIAH

Handel

Figure 47

understand the music he is to perform, know what he wants to accomplish from an interpretative standpoint and then convey his wishes to the group under his direction by every means at his command. It is not enough for him to know how he wants a composition to sound if he cannot impart his ideas to those under his direction. For example, if the mood is quiet, as in the Debussy Prélude à l'après-midi d'un faune, (See Figure 48), or the beautiful adagio movement of the Schumann SYMPHONY No. 2, C Major, Op. 61 a quiet, reserved beat will portray the soft, delicate style required. This smooth, relaxed motion must remain at all times precise and easily "read".

Just the opposite is true in conducting a vigorous work. The entire body should enter into the beat pattern when conducting music of an energetic, forte style such as the FINALE of the SYMPHONY NO. 4, (F) minor, Op. 36 by Tchaikovsky or the opening bars of Wagner's PRELUDE TO DIE MEISTERSINGER. (See Figure 49). The body will move then in a coordinated fashion from the feet and ankles through the knees and waist to the shoulders, arms, and head. Remember that a vigorous beat must not become a stiff, unrelaxed and awkward motion.

PRÉLUDE
a
l'après-midi d'un faune.

CLAUDE DEBUSSY

Figure 48

THE MASTERSINGERS OF NUREMBERG
(*Die Meistersinger von Nuernberg*)
(*Overture*)

Richard Wagner
1813-1883

Figure 49

CHAPTER IV
The Five Beat Measure

This beat figure is very much like the six bar pattern in execution, so no detailed explanation is necessary. If the six bar beat has been mastered the five beat will not be particularly difficult to learn. The same rules of relaxation, precision, grace, proper placement and proportion of the motions used, as in previous study, must be followed.

The five beat is not encountered as frequently as some others but it is found in scores often enough to require the conductor to be thoroughly at home in executing it. The five beat patterns most often used are diagrammed in Figures 50 and 51 and are the ones recommended for students.

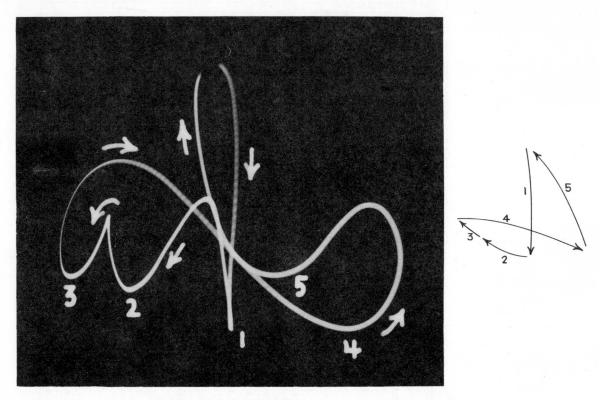

Figure 50. The Five Beat.

Figure 52 from the Hanson SYMPHONY No. 1, E minor, Op. 21 (NORDIC) may be best conducted by using the five figure in Figure 51. This pattern, as diagrammed in Figure 54, could also be employed here.

There are other ways of doing five. Occasionally, when the rhythm divides into a definite 2 and 3 beat pattern or a 3 and 2 beat pattern and continues for some time, it may be convenient to resort to one of the five beats diagrammed in Figures 53 and 54.

It will be seen that these two diagrams are actually a combination of the three and two figures already studied. Notice in Figure 53 that the last two beats are higher and not as large as the first three. This pattern separates beats, 1, 2 and 3 distinctly from beats 4 and 5 because of the rhythmic division of this measure. In the two and three pattern

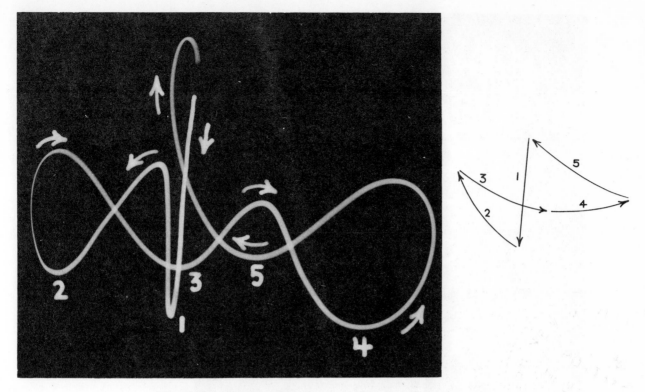

Figure 51. The Five Beat.

SYMPHONY NO. 1, E MINOR, Op. 21
(Nordic)
Animato　　　　　　　　　　　Movement I　　　　　　　　　　　Hanson

50747　　Figure 52

(Figure 54) the same plan is followed for the same reason. A classic example of the five measure sometimes done in this latter fashion is found in the second movement of the Tchaikovsky SYMPHONY NO. 6, B minor, Op. 74 (Figure 55). After the tempo has been established many conductors execute this movement by employing the two beat conventional pattern with the downward motion indicating the first two counts of the bar and by stretching the upward movement enough to contain the elapsed time of the last three beats. FETES by Debussy (Figure 56) is a musical example of the five beat in combination of three and two.

THE SEVEN BEAT MEASURE

This beat is usually done one of the three ways diagrammed in Figures 57 and 59. See musical example in Figure 58.

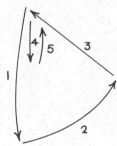

Figure 53. The Five Beat.

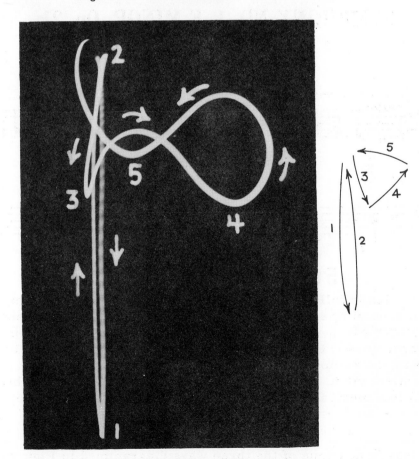

Figure 54. The Five Beat.

SYMPHONY NO. 6, B MINOR, Op. 74

(Pathétique)
Movement II

Allegro con grazia

Tchaikovsky

Figure 55

FETES

Animé et très rythmé

Debussy

Figure 56

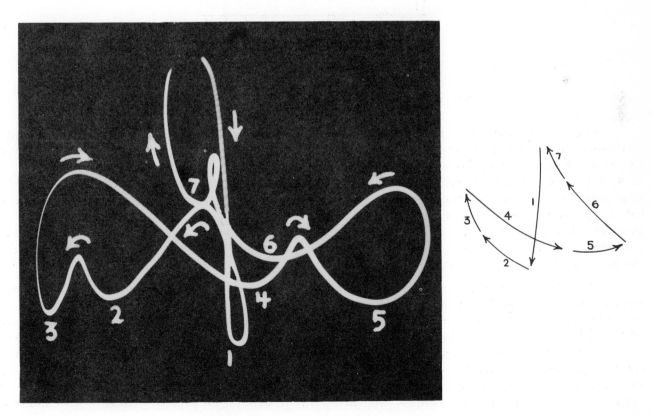

Figure 57

SYMPHONY NO. 1, E MINOR, Op. 21

(Nordic)

Poco meno mosso

Movement I

Hanson

Figure 58

As this measure is a combination of three and four, the conductor may note whether the division is three and then four or the opposite and conduct it accordingly, using the conventional three and four patterns in combination. When the seven beat is executed in this manner the same rule applies as in doing the five bar in regard to making the second beat group somewhat smaller than the first for the sake of clarity. Sometimes the composer places a dotted line between the notes of the bar to assist the conductor and players, as follows:

THE NINE AND TWELVE BEAT MEASURES

These beat patterns are actually the three and four beat bars sub-divided. The main rhythmic divisions of the measure are set off by broad, definite motions. In the nine beat bar these broad motions occur on counts 1, 4 and 7. In the twelve beat bar they occur on 1, 4, 7 and 10. The intervening beats in each instance are done mainly with the wrist. In studying the diagrams of these beat patterns, in Figures 60 and 61, observe the direction taken by each of these short, intervening beats between the main rhythmic divisions of the bar. If the tempo is too fast for clarity in a nine or twelve bar, when directed as diagrammed in Figures 60 and 61, change to the conventional three and four measure pattern. Study musical Figures 62 and 63.

The student should be aware of the fact that there are times in conducting contemporary music when 3, 5 and 7 bars must be contracted into combinations of one, two and three motions with the elapsed time length of the beats within the bar being unequal in the case of 5 and 7. These time signatures are scattered through scores when they are employed and, to make matters more complicated, are often preceded and followed by a mixture of the more conventional time signatures. It is suggested that the young conductor, though he may never use these difficult combinations, work on them for the reason that by so doing he will improve his basic baton technique. At this point it will be helpful to practice all fundamental beats, changing from one to another without interruption.

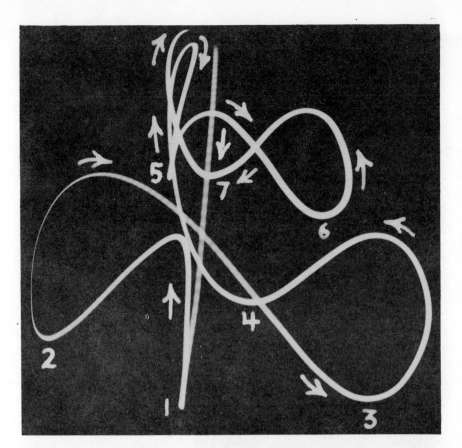

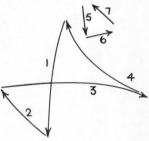

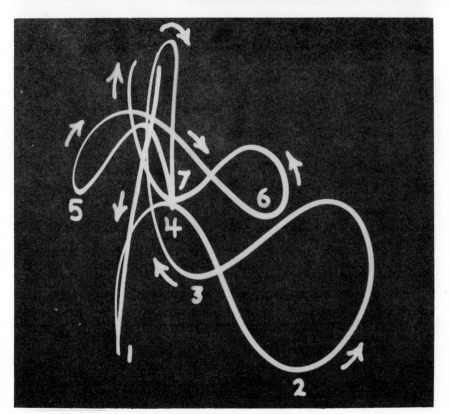

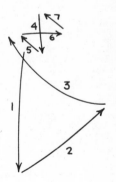

Figure 59. Seven Beat.

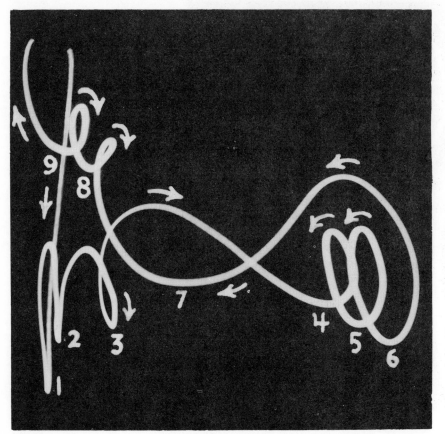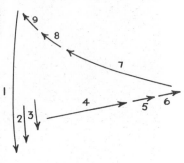

Figure 60. Nine Beat.

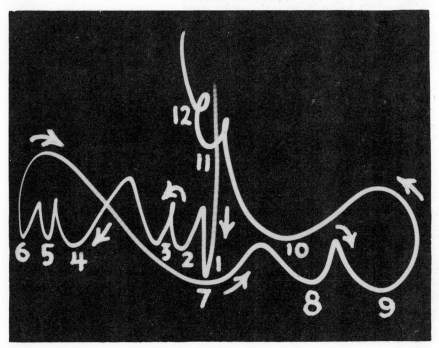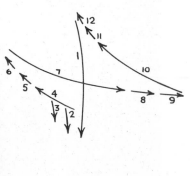

Figure 61. Twelve Beat.

Tres moderé **PRÉLUDE À L'APRÈS - MIDI D'UN FAUNE** Debussy

Figure 62

Tres lent **PRÉLUDE À L'APRÈS - MIDI D'UN FAUNE** Debussy

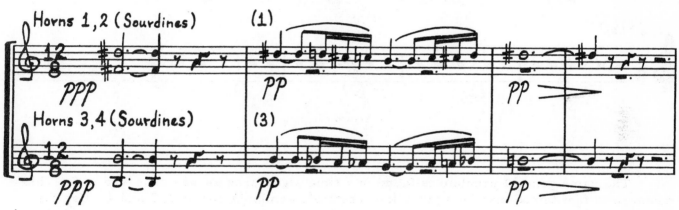

Figure 63

The following exercises will serve as models for drill. Others may be invented if further study is desired. It is advisable to think of the eighth note as the basic unit of measure. Counting aloud during initial practice may be of considerable assistance.

The execution of the 3/8 bars in Figure 64 is exactly the same as the one in a bar beat already studied. The 3 in one is not particularly difficult by itself but becomes so when preceded and followed by other time signatures.

The rapid 5 bar may be divided into 2 and 3 or 3 and 2. Conduct it by using the conventional two beat pattern but lengthen the total elapsed time of one of the motions to include the extra eighth note. The result is an irregular two measure. The actual distance covered by each beat is the same but one is more rapid than the other.

Figure 64

Figures in parentheses indicate the number of beats in the bar.

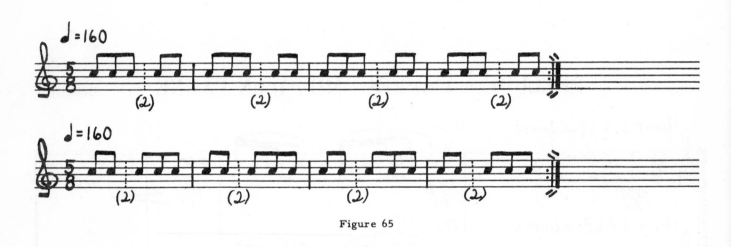

Figure 65

The same general problem is found in 7 time signatures as was observed in 5. This measure in fast tempo may be divided into rhythmic combinations of 2, 3 and 4. Use the basic two beat pattern with one motion slower than the other to accommodate the added note when the bar division is in two sections or the three beat pattern when the measure division is in three parts.

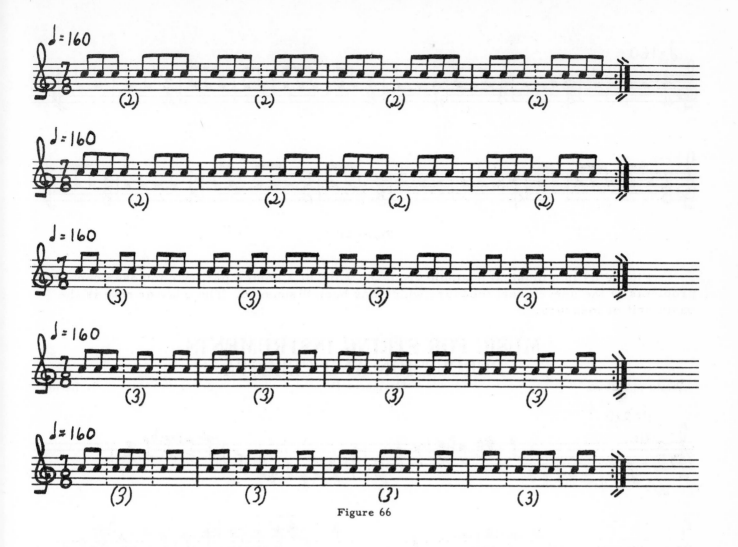

Figure 66

Combine several or all of these time signatures and their various possibilities as in Figure 67.

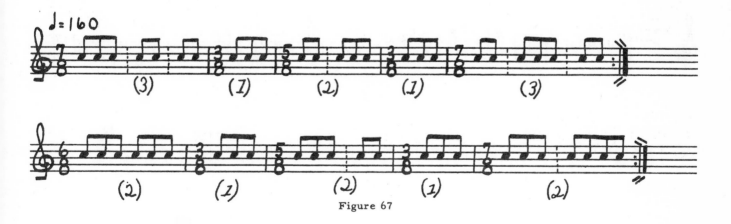

Figure 67

Add the conventional time signatures as found in Figure 68.

Figure 68

Figure 69 is a musical example from the work of a contemporary composer containing problems of the uneven beat measure which has been discussed. The quarter note is the basic unit of measure.

MUSIC FOR STRING INSTRUMENTS
PERCUSSION AND CELESTA

Presto strepitoso   Movement IV   Bartok

Figure 69

CHAPTER V
The Use of the Left Hand

It has often been said that a poor conductor is one whose left hand does what his right hand does. It is very true that some conductors use the left hand excessively for marking the beat pattern. However, there can be great misunderstanding regarding this question of the use of the left hand. The meaning of the above mentioned criticism is not that the left hand must hang at the conductor's side most of the time but that it is not employed often enough for the four main uses for which it is fitted. The left hand should be used for:

(1) cueing
(2) dynamics
(3) emphasis
(4) clarity

In order that the left hand function easily and gracefully when it is needed for these four uses it is best that it be in a position of readiness. This is accomplished by using it in conjunction with the right hand to mark the beat pattern. There are exceptions to all rules, of course. In a passage such as the opening bars of the SYMPHONY NO. 94 IN G MAJOR by Haydn "Surprise" (Figure 70) the calm, quiet mood demanded may be best obtained and even emphasized by keeping the left hand motionless at one's side. Such instances where the left hand is not needed for some specific use are not, relatively, very frequent in scores, however.

SYMPHONY NO. 94, G MAJOR
(Surprise)

Adagio cantabile   Movement I   Haydn

Figure 70

Let us examine each of the four uses of the left hand: CUEING

To cue means to indicate to a player or players who have been resting when they should resume playing. Cueing is not only a reminder. It also insures a unified entrance when a number of performers or an entire section are concerned. The number of cues given in any composition will vary with different conductors. Certain general rules may help the student in making his decisions in this regard as follows:

(1) If very limited time has been given to the rehearsal of a work it may be necessary to give more cues than if the composition has been rehearsed thoroughly and over a long period of time.

(2) The number of bars a performer or section has rested must be considered. This may vary from a few bars to one entrance in the course of an entire movement or composition. Generally speaking, more bars may elapse without the necessity of a cue in rapid tempos than in slow movements.

(3) To secure a precise entrance cue a full section of strings, wood-wind or brass whenever possible.

(4) The individual player, if he is reliable, may often be depended upon to make his entrance unaided. In amateur and school orchestras many individuals must be cued consistently because of lack of confidence in themselves or lack of experience.

(5) There are occasions when indicating all the cues occurring in a passage may be physically impossible. The conductor must decide, in that case, which instrument or instruments are in most need of assistance. Urge the musicians under your direction to count for themselves. If they depend on some other part immediately preceding their own entrance for their cue, there could conceivably be a complete breakdown of the orchestra if the player of the part depended upon should happen to be in error.

(6) Cueing too much becomes more confusing than helpful to members of an ensemble and can distract the conductor's attention from more necessary details. Select the places to cue with care and after much study.

Cues may be given by pointing with the left hand, by a nod of the head or by simply looking toward the players concerned. Signal the cue by making an upward and forward motion if the left hand is used from a stationary position. Never nod or point at the exact moment of the entrance but, rather, give a slight preparatory upward motion with the head or arm.

If the left hand is marking the beat pattern at the moment the cue is given, reach out and toward those concerned with an emphatic gesture. Anticipate all cues by looking toward the performers involved in order that they may have ample warning. Once a cue has been made, the conductor should give his attention to other matters unless he wishes to help the players just cued for reasons of phrasing, dynamics, rhythm or emphasis.

Do in rehearsal what you intend to do in performance. Always indicate the same cues in the same manner. You will avoid accidents in public performance by so doing. Practice cueing by conducting imaginary problems. For example, imagine yourself conducting a four-four allegro. Cue the brass on the second beat of the third bar and the timpani on the first beat of the fourth bar. See Figure 71.

Figure 71

Compose and practice similar problems in varying tempos, making them as simple or complex as desired. It is suggested that careful study of Chapter XI, Seating the Orchestra, should take place before attempting these exercises, for the conductor must have a mental picture of the orchestra's seating plan and look in the direction of the proper section or individual as he gives his cue both in practice and in an actual rehearsal situation. Learning to look away from the score is, possibly, the hardest thing for student conductors to master.

DYNAMICS:

Dynamics may be indicated with either or both hands. However, the left hand is the most effective instrument for conveying to the performers the dynamic changes as they occur in a work. This motion may be directed to cover the entire orchestra or only a particular player or players.

Let us examine the technique used in indicating the dynamic markings found in the average score:

P Hold the left hand still, palm open in preparatory beat position. Lean away from the orchestra for all P and PP effects. Figure 72.

Figure 72

Figure 73

PP Extend the arm full length straight forward from P position with the palm in the same position as in P.

Figure 74

PPP Raise the arm to a level with the head or a little above, palm still open and facing the orchestra. Figure 74.

F, FF and FFF Fortes are indicated by a broader, more vigorous beat with the left hand as well as with the right. The fists should be closed and the body should lean toward the ensemble. Keep the arms further from the body in fortes than in pianos. Don't conduct a forte passage timidly. Use the body freely, moving the legs, waist, shoulders and head smoothly and gracefully in conjunction with the arms. Figure 75.

Figure 75

SFZ (sforzando) Indicate this sign by moving the left hand, fist closed, in a sharp, rapid and vigorous motion either from a preparatory beat position downward or in the direction of the beat on which the sforzando falls if a beat pattern is being marked by the left hand. The amount of stress given the sforzando chord or note depends on the character of the passage and of the composition in which it occurs. Return immediately to the dynamic level of the passage after making a sforzando. In actual rehearsal the conductor will find it necessary to drill his group occasionally to insure perfect execution of both the sforzando and the forte-piano.

FP (forte-piano) This dynamic is executed forte followed always and instantly by P. It is done, also, with a rapid, vigorous motion but differs from the sforzando in that the hand opens fully as soon as the arm motion is completed to emphasize the immediate return to P.

> (Accent) Execute with a quick, authoritative motion with the wrist, though in fortissimo the accent motion may need to be almost as vigorously executed as the sforzando.

Cresc. (Crescendo) -- Dim. (Diminuendo) Indicate the crescendo by broadening the beat gradually and closing the fists as the climax is reached, especially if the dynamic level is finally a forte or fortissimo. Sometimes a gradual motion upward with the left arm, palm open and facing up, through the length of a crescendo will prove effective. This gesture is especially helpful in controlling crescendos in tympani and snare drum rolls and tremolos in the strings, if these are of short duration.

Occasionally the conductor needs to signal for more tone than he is being given in a forte or fortissimo passage. Use the left hand in this case to indicate that more tone is wanted from the players concerned. Extend the arm, palm up, moving the fingers quickly as you would if you wanted to signal someone to come to you. Turn the palm down and use a waving, good-bye motion with the hand to indicate less tone.

Many examples of dynamics may be composed for practice. Figure 76 shows one.

Figure 76

It is important that the right hand keep a steady tempo and uninterrupted beat in practicing all such examples. Work on the wrist-finger signal and the full arm up and down motion in making diminuendos and crescendos in order to establish greater left hand independence.

Conductors vary in their ability to express themselves by use of the facial muscles. Certainly every conductor should endeavor to use an expressive face in transferring, at times, the mood of the music to his instrumentalists. The foregoing dynamic indications may, in many instances, be emphasized more forcibly by this means in conjunction with the left hand.

EMPHASIS AND CLARITY:

The left hand is often used to reinforce the motion of the right hand. It may make an already vigorous right hand beat more emphatic or a marked rhythm more pronounced. It may indicate a sweeping crescendo or a broad legato style more clearly. The left hand is especially valuable for keeping the beat pattern when the conductor turns to the right on the podium to conduct an important passage played by the cellos or other instruments on that side of the orchestra. By describing the beat pattern with his left hand the conductor makes it possible for instrumentalists on his extreme left to follow him exactly even though his body may hide his right hand and arm from some of them.

Pizzicato chords are always difficult from the standpoint of precision. The left hand is of great assistance in indicating this effect. Certainly it must be remembered that a broad, slow motion in conducting pizzicato passages is dangerous. It must be borne in mind that the string player makes a pizzicato in a split second by plucking the string which is quite a different operation from that of drawing the bow to produce a tone. A sharp fleck of the conductor's wrist will usually produce the desired preciseness of ensemble. Another good method to employ in conducting pizzicato passages is that of holding the left hand high with the arm partially extended, moving the thumb and either the first or second fingers together in a rapid, pinching or snapping motion.

Independence of action is absolutely necessary if the conductor is to make full use of his left hand. In addition to the practice methods already suggested in this chapter, the student will find it helpful to conduct three with the right arm while swinging the left arm back and forth at his side in a rhythm of two. Be certain that the motion of the left arm describes a definite two rhythm while the right is doing a rhythm of three, the elapsed time being the same for both, of course. Practice, in addition, a conventional two beat with the left hand and a three beat with the right. Reverse this, doing two with the right hand and three with the left. Also practice the four measure with the right hand while the left hand does either a two or three measure in the same elapsed time. Another helpful exercise is that of making a circular motion with the left hand. Starting close to and in front of the body move the hand up and away thereby completing a full circle. Describe this motion once for each beat as a measure of three is conducted with the right hand. Do the same as four is executed. Later make the circular motion once for a complete measure of each of these two beat patterns. In this day of visual aids it may be possible to have a moving picture made of your conducting so that you can see yourself in action as the orchestra sees you.

Do not use the left hand for scratching, leaning on the music rack or fussing with your tie or coat lapel. Also, do not rest your left hand on your waist, elbow out, or put your hand in your pockets while conducting. In other words, always maintain a dignified appearance.

PART II · THEORETICAL ASPECTS

CHAPTER VI
Attributes of the Conductor

The young musician who aspires to become a conductor should have some gauge by which he may measure his qualifications in order that he may know approximately how successful he can expect to be in that profession. Conducting requires many qualities, some of which are not directly connected with his abilities as a musician. For instance, the ability to organize does not necessarily go hand-in-hand with a keen ear or a talent for score reading.

There are three general divisions into which orchestral conducting opportunities may be grouped. They are:

(1) Grade and junior high school orchestras.
(2) High school orchestras.
(3) Fine amateur, college and university, semi-professional and professional symphonies.

The student may plan to confine his conducting to the first or his ambition may be to lead a high school orchestra. Some especially talented students will surely aspire to the goal of conducting one of the many orchestras to be found in the third group. It is unlikely that any student conductor will finally be qualified to work in more than two of these orchestral conducting fields and probably will be most successful in one only. The purpose of this chapter is to acquaint him with the major qualifications necessary in each of these fields in order that he may be assisted in his study emphasis and guided in his development.

Just as we work to eliminate flaws in our technique on an instrument, so we must be aware of our strengths and weaknesses as conducting students and concentrate, especially, on the latter. The attributes listed here need no detailed explanation for understanding although they could be expanded indefinitely. Furthermore, it is certainly possible to conduct without the ultimate in ability, knowledge or fitness in the case of each item emphasized. It is equally certain that the young conductor will be more likely to succeed if he will fortify himself as strongly as possible in each category by study, self-discipline, observation, training and experience.

The grade school or junior high school conductor should have some strength in all of the following attributes:

(1) Abundant patience.
(2) Love of his work.
(3) Love of children.
(4) Ability to place himself on the child's level.
(5) Knack of maintaining discipline.
(6) Clarity of speech and expression.
(7) Sense of humor.
(8) Ability to organize the entire orchestral program.
(9) Ability to meet the public successfully.
(10) Qualities of leadership.
(11) Ability to rehearse efficiently.
(12) Spirit of cooperation and tactfulness with his superiors and fellow teachers.

(13) Fundamental knowledge of all orchestral instruments.

(14) A good sense of pitch.

(15) Adequate baton technique with emphasis on clarity of fundamental beat patterns.

If the student conductor aspires to instrumental high school conducting, these foregoing qualifications apply to him, also, with special emphasis on the following:

(5) Knack of maintaining discipline. This usually becomes much more difficult in high school.

(8) Ability to organize. The entire scope of musical activity becomes much broader and more complicated for a high school organization.

(9) Ability to meet the public successfully. The high school teacher will need to manage concert appearances, plan money-raising events, talk to parents individually and in groups and associate himself with the people of the community in many other ways.

(10) Qualities of leadership. These include such assets as aggressiveness, impressiveness, initiative, thoroughness, imagination, concentration, adaptation, and the ability to make sound decisions quickly. Such qualities are even more important in high school for the youngsters at that age need inspiration and respond more readily to a strong personality in their conductor.

(11) Ability to rehearse efficiently. Efficient rehearsing becomes more important with high school groups because of the more complicated scores used, the more complete instrumentation generally available and the more important functions before which high school instrumental groups appear, requiring more finished performances.

(13) Fundamental knowledge of all instruments. High school players will be more advanced than the beginners in grade and junior high. They will ask more difficult questions and the music they play will be more demanding technically thereby resulting in problems requiring a more specialized knowledge.

(14) A good sense of pitch. As the young player develops he should be guided in his consciousness of pitch problems. Only a conductor possessing a keen sense of pitch can provide this training.

(15) Adequate baton technique. One's baton technique must be more proficient to adequately direct the more difficult repertoire used in high school organizations.

In addition to these fifteen attributes needed by the grade and junior high school conductor, the successful high school conductor will require the following additional qualifications:

(16) Creative imagination.

(17) Ability to assemble successful programs from the standpoint of both the players and the listeners.

(18) A keen sense of rhythm.

(19) Knowledge of musical terms.

(20) Score reading ability.

The conductor who plans to go beyond public school conducting will need to possess, to a high degree, most of the foregoing attributes. This third general group of directors, those of fine amateur or professional groups, must add still further to their list of qualifications:

(21) Superior score reading ability.

(22) Exceptional innate musical talent.

(23) A long period of broad and intelligent training in all fields of music.

(24) A knowledge of the piano and preferably one orchestral instrument.

(25) Specialized training in baton technique and much actual conducting experience with live orchestras.

All this may seem discouraging to the young student. It need not be for it must be remembered that perfection in any profession comes gradually and with many years of application. It is hoped that the student may, by means of the foregoing ideas, assess himself more intelligently and thereby lay more stress on his weaknesses, strengthening these by specialized study and thought. Such study might go beyond the prescribed courses necessary for a music degree and take, for example, the form of a public speaking course, a class in acoustics or a class in the field of psychology.

CHAPTER VII
The Graceful Baton

One of the primary objectives of the arts is that of creating beauty. Beauty of line and color is striven for by the painter; beauty of form and tone by the performer of an instrument. Why, then, should the conductor be satisfied with less than a graceful baton technique? Why should he not strive for such a beat himself and teach it to his students? Yet how often such grace of line is lacking in the conductors we see today.

Recently a concert goer remarked, "I can't go to the concerts of X orchestra because I can't stand the antics of the conductor. He is so very awkward." This is an extreme attitude but how often a conductor has detracted from his performance because of his ungainly movements. Unless young conductors are made aware of this problem at the beginning of their conducting experience they are apt to develop clumsy motions and meaningless mannerisms. This often happens, for example, to high school students who are allowed to "conduct" their musical organizations. Without guidance and study they often develop beat patterns that are both awkward and difficult to read.

Becoming a capable conductor requires careful preparation and thorough musicianship for the art of the conductor embraces all music in one way or another.

The beat as it develops, may be a graceful, precise, authoritative one or it may be an awkward, aimless affair. More often than not, without proper guidance, it becomes the latter. One's conducting beat is somewhat like one's handwriting--it is peculiar to that one individual and if properly guided in the first stages of study it can be neat and beautiful and still retain the personal characteristics of the writer. If, on the other hand, a poor handwriting has been learned it is extremely difficult to correct it later in life. Likewise, a clumsy beat may never become a precise and graceful motion unless the student concerned is made aware of his faults and has the patience to correct his mistakes.

There are, of course, more important considerations in developing a baton technique than that of being graceful, but this is no excuse for allowing students to develop an unattractive beat. A good teacher of the violin, for instance, would not allow a student to stand in a slovenly position because he is too busy working on the technique of the bow arm to correct the fault in stance. Furthermore, the fact that there are a few great conductors who might better conduct behind a screen is no excuse for poor form on the part of today's student. These few men are great in spite of their faults and because of their great genius. How much greater they would have been, at least how much more pleasure they might have given their audiences, had they taken time to develop a baton technique pleasing to watch. A conductor cannot escape the spotlight and the student who aspires to be one should remember that people listen with their eyes as well as with their ears.

In several instances players have told me of having to play for some length of time under the direction of well-known conductors before they knew exactly what these men desired. The conductor with a really fine baton technique does not have to wait days or weeks to be thoroughly understood by the men under him. His beat does not confuse--it clarifies.

Occasionally one sees a concert artist whose performance is marred because of his awkward stage appearance. One surely cannot argue that his appearance would not be immeasurably improved with the addition of the grace of a Heifetz or Menuhin. Practically all students can be taught to conduct gracefully. Each will develop a style of his own, but the general pattern will remain pleasing to the eye.

In our conducting study let us keep in mind that all bodily movement must be graceful as well as authoritative, precise and without waste of motion. Let us develop an exact and dignified beat which conveys our wishes and still does not make us "pretzel" conductors or mere time-beaters.

THE PHYSICAL BATON

The size of the baton is not of vital importance, but one small in diameter, short and light is preferable to a long, heavy, thick stick. An ideal baton must be light enough to be handled with the utmost ease and for a long period of time without fatigue. For that reason the baton of wood is best. Serge Koussevitzky, for many years conductor of the Boston Symphony Orchestra, had a special baton made for his use which is ideal in every way. The following brief description may prove helpful in gauging the general size of your baton.

Mr. Koussevitzky's baton was unpainted, measured about twelve and one-half inches in length, and was tapered from about one quarter of an inch at the base to a very fine point. This baton is somewhat smaller than the average size used but it is easily seen by the players and certainly is not tiring to use nor is it the least distracting to the audience. While it is obvious that what one does with the stick is more important than its dimension or weight, still one must find a baton which feels comfortable in one's grasp and is not heavy or awkward. Certainly the "fishing pole" type of baton, long and heavy, should be avoided.

Did some one say, "Why use a baton at all?" One can find endless argument on the subject of the use of a baton versus the use of the hands only in conducting. There are a few famous conductors such as Mitropoulos and Stokowski, as well as many good choral men, who do not use a baton, but there are many more famous orchestral and choral conductors who feel that the baton is indispensable. Many maestros claim that a baton gives them a feeling of confidence and authority which they do not have when working without a stick. They maintain that it focuses their thoughts and movements in one spot. Furthermore, they feel that it represents an important contact between themselves and the members of the orchestra. The larger the ensemble concerned, the more logical this reasoning becomes. Certainly it is a more precise focal point for the eyes of the players than are the hands. A baton concentrates the gestures of the hands.

While the use of a baton is certainly considered essential by the majority of conductors, one occasionally finds a student who insists that he can do better work without it. If a student is unhappy with a stick after giving it a fair trial then he should be allowed to conduct without one, in spite of the arguments in favor of the use of a baton.

If a baton of the general size already described is not readily available, it is a simple matter to make one from a dowel which may be purchased for a few cents in any lumber yard. The application of a knife or a plane, a little sandpaper and a bit of varnish and wax will give one a baton as beautiful as any that can be purchased.

WHAT THE BATON DOES

The baton does many things through the man who controls it. It starts and stops the orchestra, band or chorus--not an easy task in itself when well done. The baton balances the tone so that the correct amount of melodic line may be heard at all times. It gives entrances and indicates rhythms where necessary. It controls crescendos and diminuendos so that they are executed smoothly and are perfectly timed. It indicates phrasing, controls tempo and tempo changes, style and color. The baton, in short, reminds the players of what they know.

Conductorless orchestras have been tried and found wanting. Rehearsing even a limited and standard repertoire has consumed too much time for the result obtained. Spontaneity of interpretation, balance and nuance are lost without a conductor. The countless subtleties which the conductor imparts to a work are found lacking. Always there has been a return to the conductor and his baton.

The conductor must remember that the orchestra desires only that he convey his wishes to them by means of a clear, concise beat. Neither the orchestra nor the audience is interested in the conductor's mannerisms. Few concert goers are impressed by the conductor who tries to attract attention to himself or who makes his work look difficult to cover his own short-comings. How calmly and quietly a great virtuoso of the violin or piano goes about his work on the concert platform. His playing is, to all appearances, effortless. He seems not to be exerting himself in the least. His energies, concentration and bodily movement are limited to the job of playing and not to needless gymnastics. The conductor likewise must make every motion count and eliminate all excess movement. When his technique is finally developed it is then his job to make each section of his group respond to his slightest wish as transferred from him to them through his baton.

CHAPTER VIII
Words and Symbols on the Score

The names of the instruments used in a composition for band or orchestra appear on the left hand margin of the first page of a score. These names may be in French, Italian, German or English depending upon where the score was originally published or the language the composer happened to prefer.. The young conductor must be familiar with these various names for he may have to answer questions in rehearsal pertaining to them. He must be quick and accurate in his answers if he is not to be embarrassed. It will be wise to study carefully the following chart and to note and remember, particularly, the names of instruments which vary markedly from the familiar English terms. The accompanying list of abbreviations will also be of assistance in marking scores.

	ABBRE-VIATIONS	ENGLISH	FRENCH	ITALIAN	GERMAN
WOOD-WIND	Pic.	Piccolo	Petite Flute	Ottavino	Kleine Flote
	Fl.	Flute	Flute	Flauto	Flote
	Ob.	Oboe	Hautbois	Oboe	Oboe
	E. H.	English-Horn	Cor anglais	Corno Inglese	Englisches Horn
	Cl.	Clarinet	Clarinette	Clarinetto	Klarinette
	B. Cl.	Bass-clarinet	Clarinette basse	Clarinetto Basso	Bass Klarinette
	Bn.	Bassoon	Basson	Fagotto	Fagott
	D. Bn.	Double-bassoon	Contre-basson	Contrafagotto	Kontrafagott
BRASS	Hn.	Horn	Cor	Corno	Horn
	Trpt.	Trumpet	Trompette	Tromba	Trompete
	Trb.	Trombone	Trombone	Trombone	Posaune
	Tb.	Tuba	Tuba basse	Tuba	Bass Tuba
PER-CUS-SION	K. D.	Kettledrums	Timbales	Timpani	Pauken
	S. D.	Side-drum	Tambour	Tamburo militare	Kleine Trommel
	B. D.	Bass-drum	Grosse caisse	Gran cassa	Grosse Trommel
	Cym.	Cymbals	Cymbales	Piatti or Cinelli	Becken
	Bls.	Bells	Gloches	Campanelle	Glocken
	Glk.	Glockenspiel	Carillon	Campanetta	Glockenspiel
	Δ	Triangle	Triangle	Tringolo	Triangel
	Tmb.	Tambourine	Tambour de basque	Tamburino	Tambourin
	O	Gong	Tam-tam	Tam-tam	Tam-tam
	Cst.	Castanets	Castagnettes	Castagnettes	Kastagnetten
	Xly.	Xylophone	Xylophon	Zilafone	Xylophon
	Cel.	Celesta	Celeste	Celesta	Celeste
	Hp.	Harp	Harpe	Arpa	Harfe
STRINGS	V.	Violin	Violon	Violino	Violine (or Geige)
	Va.	Viola	Alto	Viola	Bratsche
	Vcl.	Violoncello	Violoncelle	Violoncello	Violoncell
	D. B.	Double-bass	Contre-basse	Contrabasso	Kontrabass

The conductor who is properly prepared should be familiar with the meaning of symbols which are most often found in scores. They are as important to the conductor as shorthand symbols are to the stenographer. The following is a list of those commonly encountered:

8 va. ∿∿∿	-- To be played an octave higher than written.
8 basso ∿∿∿	-- To be played an octave lower than written.
♩♩ ♩♩♩ ♩♩♩♩♩	-- A couplet, triplet or quintuplet; a group of notes of equal value to be sounded within the basic rhythm of the measure.
⁄.	-- Repetition of the measure preceding.
⁄⁄.	-- Repeat the last two bars.
' // ✓	-- A breathing place or break in the music.
a¹	-- One player on a part.
a²	-- Two players on a part.
a³	-- Three players on a part.
♯	-- Tremolo, which is done by means of a short, fast, repeated movement of the bow.
♯	-- Play sixteenth notes.
tr. ∿∿∿	-- Trill.
Como prima	-- As before.
D. S.	-- Del segno; return to the sign (·§· or :§:) and repeat.
D. C.	-- Return to the beginning.
Mute or Sordino	-- A device placed on the bridge of string instruments or in the bell of brass instruments to dampen the tone.
Solo	-- As an orchestral direction, Solo (or simply I) marks a passage where one instrument takes a leading part.
Soli	-- The leading part to be played by more than one player. Often used following the "Solo" indication to signify that an entire section is to play again.
Con sordini	-- With mute.
Senza sordini	-- Without mute.
Bouche, stopped or +	-- Complete closing of the bell of the French horn with the hand.
Cuivre	-- Brassy.
Senza couvert or O	-- Open. Remove the mute or the hand from brass instrument.
♩	-- Use an open (unstopped) string or play harmonic.
Pizz.	-- Pizzicato; the string is set in vibration not by the bow but by being plucked with the fingers of the right hand. When occasionally the left hand is used for pizzicato this is indicated by the sign + over the notes concerned.

Arco	-- Use the bow again following pizzicato.
Ponticello	-- Play close to the bridge with the bow.
Col legno or CL	-- Play with the wood of the bow instead of the bow hair.
Sul tasto, flautando or sur la touche	-- Play on the fingerboard with the bow.
Pousse or V	-- Up bow.
Tirez or Π	-- Down bow.
Tacet	-- Silent.
Tutti or F.O.	-- Whole; all; full orchestra.
G. P.	-- Grand pause.
Vi-de	-- Cut from vi to de.
V. S.	-- Turn page immediately.
Segue	-- Immediately.
Divisi	-- Players divide into two or more parts, hitherto having played in unison.
Unis	-- Unison; no longer divisi.
Alla corda	-- On the string

CHAPTER IX
Setting Tempos - - Tempo Terms
Dynamic Markings

Tempo means, in music, the speed or speeds at which a composition is to be performed. Although the tempo of a work often varies during the course of a composition it is extremely important that the basic or beginning speed be set with great care. The conductor has the entire responsibility for this and must take into consideration all factors which can help him in making his initial tempo selection. While all of these may not be present in any one composition, there are four main ideas to assist the conductor in setting tempos:

(1) Tradition.
(2) Tempo indications.

(3) Metronome markings.
(4) Over-all timing.

Unfortunately some of these aids are not always to be relied upon which makes the task of the conductor that much greater. Let us discuss each of these tempo-setting factors in turn:

(1) TRADITION:

According to the dictionary tradition is the "transmission of knowledge, doctrines, customs, etc. from generation to generation". According to this definition it might be assumed that the main tempos of, for instance, a work such as Schubert's SYMPHONY NO. 8 in B minor, (UNFINISHED) would be based on tradition and would always be alike as set by great conductors of today. This is not the case, however, for every conductor injects his own "feeling" for the music into his interpretations and no two men will "feel" this symphony, or any other composition, alike. For this reason there may occur variation of tempo in some instances as one conductor's conception of a work is compared to that of another.

If the young conductor is to hear a composition which he is to conduct with the idea of ascertaining the "traditional" tempos, he should listen, when possible, to more than one version of a work as played by recognized conductors. This is difficult to do any other way than by means of recordings and even then it may not be possible in many instances. However, the inexperienced conductor has no other choice unless he wishes to accept the tempo ideas of one man and copy his tempos as exactly as possible. By listening to two or more versions of a work the young conductor will have a better idea of what traditional tempos are even though the versions he hears will not exactly agree. He will then be better prepared to set a speed which seems natural and logical to him.

It is perfectly possible that he might, otherwise, without having had enough background and experience, decide upon a tempo which would be entirely outside the limits of good taste. In listening to records it is wise to be certain that the recording machine being used is set at the proper speed. Sometimes, too, tempos are distorted by conductors in making recordings when they slow or hasten the tempo of a composition because of the necessity of fitting it into a prescribed amount of record space--another reason for hearing more than one interpretation where records are used for study. There is a possibility that the long play records will tend to eliminate this reason for such occasional altering of tempos in recordings.

(2) TEMPO INDICATIONS:

The terms allegro, andante, largo and other similar ones give the conductor a general idea of what the composer wanted in tempo but are not definite enough to go beyond that.

Such terms indicate the spirit of a work as much as the speed. They are a welcome aid in making a choice of tempo but are not a definite or precise indication. Every conductor must study carefully tempo terms, however, until their meaning is thoroughly learned.

(3) METRONOME MARKINGS:

Metronome markings indicate the kind of note which receives one beat and the number of beats to be indicated per minute. They are valuable aids in setting tempos but are not, by any means, invariably correct. (Figure 77).

Signature 4/4	Metronome Marking $\quad \downarrow = 60$	Conductor beats four to one bar at a speed of 60 per minute.
Signature 6/8	Metronome Marking $\quad \downarrow = 96$	Conductor beats six to one bar at a speed of 96 per minute.
Signature 3/4	Metronome Marking $\quad \downarrow . = 120$	Conductor beats one to one bar at a speed of 120 per minute.

Figure 77

Metronome markings in the classic works are sometimes unreliable and not according to "tradition", while in later compositions, especially contemporary ones conductors sometimes ignore metronomic indications completely. It is advisable for every conductor to own a metronome, preferably the electric type. Test any metronome occasionally to be sure that it is accurate, especially the older model with the sliding lead weight. The conductor must practice setting tempos with the metronome until he is able to gauge very closely if not exactly all metronomic indications. It may help him to recall tunes which fit some of the key speeds, for instance, the Sousa STARS AND STRIPES FOREVER which is generally done at a speed of $\quad \downarrow = 120$

(4) OVER-ALL TIMING:

The films, radio and television fields demand that the conductor be able to set a tempo or tempos within seconds of the same speed every time he performs a composition. The conductor must be especially adept at setting tempos if he plans to work in these fields. As a result of the need for exact timing composers are more and more printing on the score the over-all timing of a composition. It is a simple matter for the young conductor to get out his watch or a stop watch and check his over-all timing results with those of the composer.

In the final analysis individual judgment, tempered by the aids already discussed, must be the decisive factor in setting all tempos. Individual judgment is the "feeling" of the conductor for correct tempo. It is somewhat of a sixth sense--an intangible ability which some musicians have more decidedly than others. It cannot be taught and it is impossible to describe. Experience, hearing much music and thorough study in all fields of music develop this innate feeling for or sense of tempo but the talent must already be present to a marked degree.

The problem in regard to tempo, then, is that of setting the main speed of a movement or composition, of changing speed smoothly and logically as the need arises and then of returning again to the original tempo whenever necessary. It is naturally true that in many cases there is no indication for change of speed at any time in the course of a movement or composition. However, the young conductor will be surprised how difficult it is to maintain a steady tempo once it is acceptably set. This particular problem is not easier when one actually stands before a large body of players for then there are numerous distractions, possible nervousness on the part of the conductor and the players, and other causes for unconscious alteration of tempo not the least of which is the tendency of most ensembles to drag slow, pianissimo passages and to rush forte, rapid places in the score.

Before deciding on a tempo hum the bars involved, play them on the piano or hear them played by experienced conductors in recordings, on the radio or by a live orchestra. Take into consideration all other aids at hand and then set your tempo as you "feel" it.

The following lists of tempo terms and dynamic markings are in common usage and must be part of the equipment of every conductor. Others which are sometimes found in scores will be defined in any good music dictionary.

TEMPO TERMS

Very slowest tempo:
  larghissimo
  adagissimo
  lentissimo

Very slow tempo:
  largo
  adagio
  lento

Slow tempo:
  adagietto
  larghetto

Moderately slow tempo:
  andante
  andantino

Moderate tempo:
  moderato

Moderately Rapid Tempo:
  allegro
  allegretto (slower than allegro)

Very rapid tempo:
  vivo
  vivace
  presto

Most rapid possible tempo:
  prestissimo
  vivacissimo

TERMS FOR TEMPO VARIATIONS

Gradual acceleration:
  accelerando
  stringendo
  poco a poco animato

Immediately faster:
  piu allegro
  piu presto
  piu animato
  piu mosso
  piu tosto
  piu stretto

Gradual ritard:
  ritardando
  rallentando

Immediately slower:
  piu lento
  meno mosso
  ritenuto

Slower tempo with an increase in power:
  allargando

Slower tempo with a decrease in power:
  morendo
  calando
  smorzando

VARIABLE TEMPO INDICATIONS

tempo rubato . . . . robbed time; flexible
ad libitum . . . . at pleasure
a piacere . . . . at pleasure
a capriccio . . . . at the caprice
recitative . . . . free in tempo and rhythm
tempo giusto . . . . steady tempo

QUALIFYING TEMPO EXPRESSIONS

a tempo . . . . at preceding rate of speed
tempo I . . . . at original speed
non troppo . . . . not too much
ma non troppo . . . . but not too much
lunga . . . . long
misurato . . . . strict time
moto . . . . motion
a poco . . . . a little
subito . . . . immediately
molto . . . . much
assai . . . . very
Doppio movimente . . . . double movement of time, that is, twice as fast.
meno . . . . less

QUALIFYING TERMS SOMETIMES COUPLED
WITH TEMPO INDICATIONS

agitato . . . . agitated
cantabile . . . . singable
furioso . . . . wild
grave . . . . heavy; serious
pesante . . . . firm; vigorous; heavy
marcato . . . . marked; distinct
sostenuto . . . . sustained
tenuto . . . . held for full value of note
tranquillo . . . . quietly
maestoso . . . . majestic; dignified
expressive . . . . with expression
con brio . . . . with brilliancy
con fuoco . . . . with fire
con passione . . . . with passion
con grazia . . . . with grace
con tenerezza . . . . with tenderness
dolce . . . . gently; sweetly
giocoso . . . . humorously
pastorale . . . . in simple style
scherzando . . . . jokingly
sotto voce . . . . with subdued voice

DYNAMICS MARKINGS

pianississimo (ppp) . . . . softly as possible
pianissimo (pp) . . . . very softly
piano (p) . . . . softly
piu piano . . . . more softly
il piu piano . . . . most softly
piano assai . . . . very softly
mezzo-piano (mp) . . . . moderately softly
forte (f) . . . . loudly
fortissimo (ff) . . . . very loudly
fortississimo (fff) . . . . loudly as possible
piu forte . . . . more loudly
il piu forte . . . . most loudly
mezzo forte (mf) . . . . moderately loud

DYNAMICS MARKINGS (Cont.)

forte-piano (fp) . . . . loudly followed immediately by softly

sforzando (sf or sfz). . . . . accent a single note or chord, the

forzato (fz) . . . . amount of stress depending upon the character
of the passage and of the composition.

rinforzando (rinf). . . . . increase in power extending through phrase
or passage.

crescendo. . . . . gradually becoming louder

decrescendo . . . . gradually becoming softer

diminuendo . . . . gradually becoming softer

CHAPTER X
Clefs and Transpositions

CLEFS

At one time the Great Staff sufficed for all tones emitted by voices of average range. (See Figure 78.) Voices were not trained and were practically the only means of musical expression.

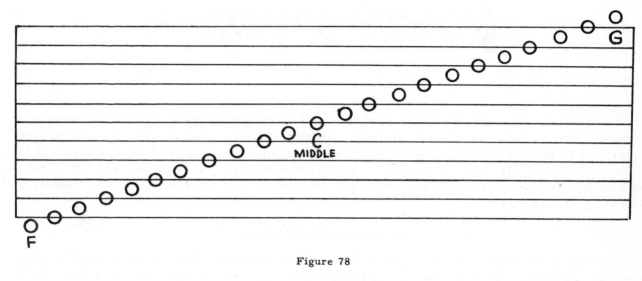

Figure 78

In order to help the vocalists to find tones they were to sing, the Gothic letters G, F, C were placed on the staff. These have gradually become our present day 𝄞 , 𝄢 and 𝄡 clefs. Later the Great Staff was broken into staves of five leger lines for each voice to simplify the reading of each part. When the Great Staff was divided eight clefs resulted as shown in Figure 79.

Figure 79

Four of these clefs are used today:

(1) Treble or G clef.
 The line of the staff denoted by this clef is G.

(2) Bass or F clef.
 The line of the staff denoted by this clef is F.

(3) Alto or C clef, third line.
 The line of the staff denoted by this clef is middle C.

(4) Tenor or C clef, fourth line.
 The line of the staff denoted by this clef is middle C.

Figure 80

Some of the instruments of the orchestra use only one of these clefs while others use two, three and, in the case of the trombone, all four of them. The conductor must be able to name the note being played by any one instrument at any time and for that reason must be as at home in reading all four clefs as the players themselves. Practice reading the parts on a score which employs the clefs with which you are unfamiliar until you can read rapidly and accurately all four clefs.

TRANSPOSITIONS

Transpositions are usually difficult for the student conductor to understand and remember. The basic principles are simple, however. If these are learned and some time is given to practice in working actual exercises in transposition there should be no problem in regard to this phase in the student's preparation.

Orchestral instruments are built to sound in one particular key. The instruments built in C, with four exceptions, are non-transposing instruments while all the others are transposing ones. The four exceptions are the glockenspiel, C piccolo, contra bassoon and the bass viol. These four transpose one octave (see Figure 81). The glockenspiel and C piccolo sound one octave higher than written and the contra bassoon and bass viol one octave lower. All the other transposing instruments are named for the key in which they are built as, for example, the A trumpet or the F horn. If the note C is taken as a standard or starting point we see that when the A trumpet plays this written note it sounds in the key of the instrument or a minor third lower.

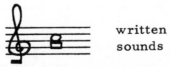

written
sounds

A trumpet

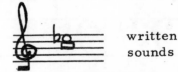

written
sounds

To sound C the note E^b must be written, a minor third higher.

This relationship between the written note and the note which actually sounds maintains throughout the range of the A clarinet. All orchestral instruments with five exceptions sound down from the printed note in like manner with the interval changing depending on the key name of the instrument in question. The F horn, for example, will sound F when reading C, one fifth lower.

F horn

To sound C the part for this instrument must be written a fifth higher.

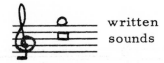

     Three trumpets transpose up from C. They are the D, E , and F trumpets. If these three, plus the piccolo and glockenspiel are remembered as transposing up from C it is then not difficult to identify those which transpose down--namely, all the remaining transposing instruments of the orchestra.

     The conductor must be careful how he expresses himself in asking a player of a transposing instrument for a specified pitch. If he wants the A clarinetist to sound the pitch C he must ask for "concert" C, otherwise the player will play written C and the pitch sounded will be A, a minor third lower. Always preface the pitch name with the word "concert" in asking for a definite pitch. For comparison with the score the conductor may want to know what the printed note on the A clarinetist's part is. In that case ask him for the "printed" or "written" note in question.

     The chart in Figure 81 lists the transposing instruments of the orchestra. The whole note indicates the note written and the square note the pitch sounded.

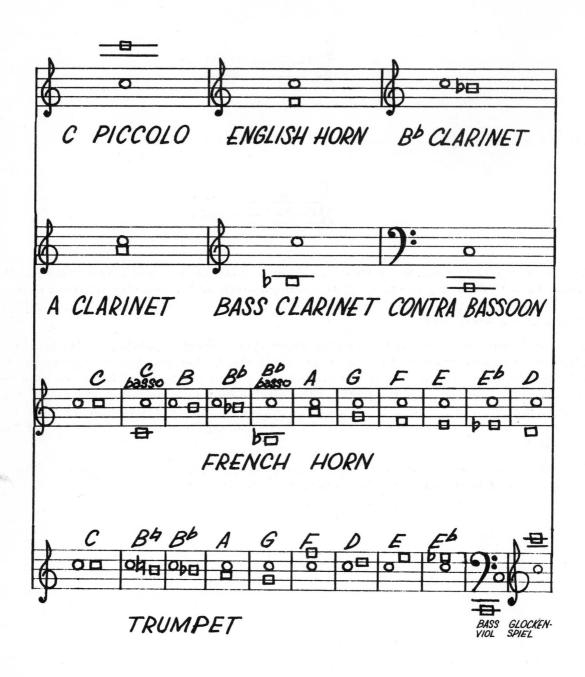

Figure 81

CHAPTER XI
Seating the Orchestra

Over the years there has been much experimentation in search of an acoustically better seating arrangement for the symphony orchestra. One of the notable leaders in these experiments has been Leopold Stokowski, for many years conductor of the Philadelphia Orchestra. However, the general arrangement of the choirs of the orchestra has remained unchanged and is fairly well standardized. In Figure 82 the seating arrangement most often used is charted.

Variations from this arrangement occur primarily in the string section. The first violins are never moved from their position outside and to the left of the conductor but the second violins, violas and cellos are sometimes interchanged. As the violin is smaller in size than the other strings and has a correspondingly smaller tone, and as the first and second violin parts are generally closely allied it is wise to keep the second violins on the left of the conductor. This has the advantages of unifying the violins and of placing their f-holes toward the audience for maximum volume of tone.

The bass viol section is most often found back of the cellos for the reason that they play identical or similar parts so much of the time. This plan, however, is not followed invariably. When the bass section is moved to the left the percussion group is then changed from the left rear to the right rear.

The wood-wind remain as charted in all cases. In seating the wood-wind place the first players in a box position in the center of the section so that they are in close contact with each other. This results in better leadership for the wood-wind group as a whole particularly as regards phrasing ideas, intonation and ensemble. The horns must be seated close to the wood-wind players, for their parts, from a musical and orchestration standpoint, are so often closely related to those of the latter.

The trombones and trumpets are sometimes seen in a straight line with the trumpets outside. Group first chair brass players as close to one another as possible.

The percussion section may be moved to the center or right side of the stage but the position in the chart in Figure 82 is the one most often used.

The seating arrangement for smaller orchestral groups than the complete symphony must be left to the judgment of the conductor and is primarily dependent on the number and kinds of players available. A balanced, pleasing appearance must be achieved in any case. For example, if the viola and cello sections are small, a better visual result may be achieved by placing the second violins to the conductor's right with the violas and cellos inside the two violin groups. In this arrangement the violas will sound fuller if placed on the inside left of the conductor with their f-holes facing in the direction of the audience. Figure 83 shows another possibility for use when the violins are not numerous enough to divide. In this instance the violas and cellos sit on the right with the violas first and the cellos at their rear. An extremely limited number of strings may require the seating plan in Figure 84. The use of the piano is, of course, optional depending upon the number and capabilities of the students in the orchestra. When it is used it will look better to the left and inside the violins if an upright type instrument. In the charts given it is placed in front of the conductor, assuming it to be a grand piano, because it is so often depended upon for leadership in a small ensemble. It may be to the left rear if this is not as essential regardless of the type of instrument in use.

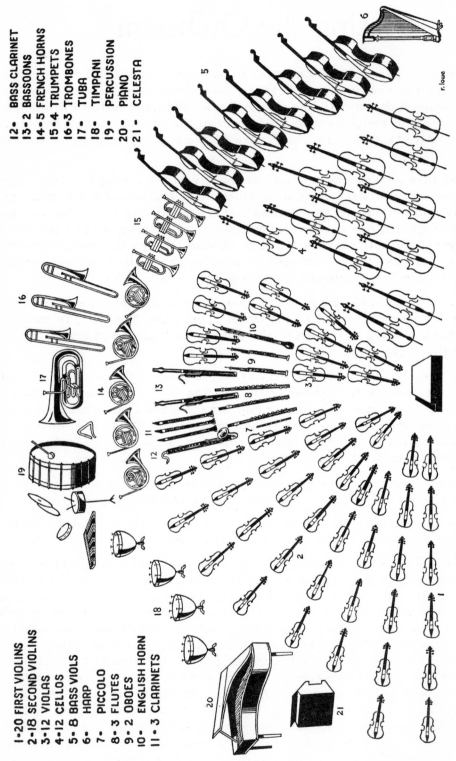

1-20 FIRST VIOLINS
2-18 SECOND VIOLINS
3-12 VIOLAS
4-12 CELLOS
5- 8 BASS VIOLS
6- HARP
7- PICCOLO
8- 3 FLUTES
9- 2 OBOES
10- ENGLISH HORN
11- 3 CLARINETS

12- BASS CLARINET
13- 2 BASSOONS
14-5 FRENCH HORNS
15-4 TRUMPETS
16-3 TROMBONES
17- TUBA
18- TIMPANI
19- PERCUSSION
20- PIANO
21- CELESTA

r. lowe

DRAKE-DES MOINES SYMPHONY ORCHESTRA

SEATING PLAN

Figure 82

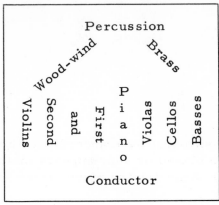

Figure 83

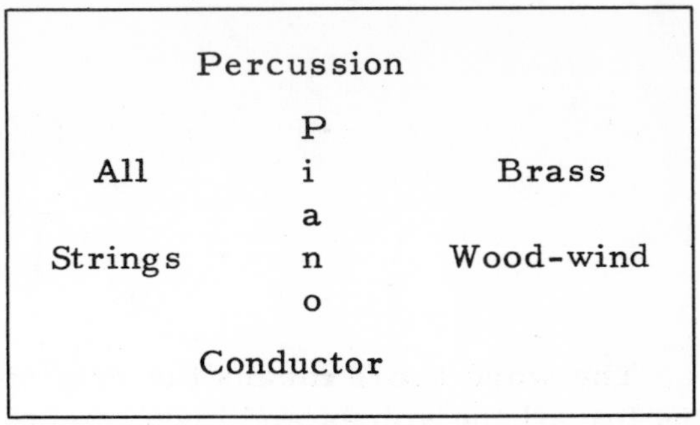

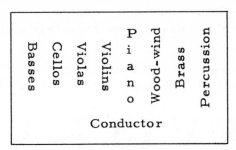

Figure 84

There is an additional advantage for the school orchestra over the professional symphony in having the violins together, for often the second section is weak or at least is partially made up of timid or inexperienced players. When these players are not in an exposed position in relation to the audience and are near stronger players they do better work.

Orchestras for opera, musical and minstrel shows, plays and the like are seated with the strings on the conductor's left and the wood-wind, brass and percussion on the right with the piano, if one is used, in front of the conductor. This seating is necessary because of the long, narrow pit usually provided for such orchestras. See Figure 85.

Figure 85

CHAPTER XII
The Score

The word score means the original draft of a composition or its transcript, with the parts for all the voices and instruments. Every note to be played or sung appears on this score so that the conductor may see at a glance any detail of the notated music which he wishes to read or check. (See Figure 89 on page 73)

Unfortunately it is not always possible to buy or rent a full score, for many short and comparatively unimportant compositions are not published with full score. In this case piano reductions (Figure 86) or condensed versions (Figure 87) must be used but these are not recommended if a full score is available, for only with full score can the conductor do a thorough job of rehearsing and directing the performance of a work. It will be noted that the condensed score is more detailed than the piano reduction version. More and more compositions suitable for public school performance are being published with full score. The public school conductor can, by exercising care, select programs for which most or all the music chosen will have the very necessary complete score. The works played by the full-fledged symphony orchestras are almost without exception available with full score, either the small miniature score or the larger and more expensive score. The latter differs from the miniature version only in size and has the one advantage of being somewhat easier to read.

Do not confuse the word score with the loosely used word "music". The "music" exists only as sound. Nor should we refer to the score when we mean the parts. The parts are the

SEVILLA

Arranged by FELIX GUENTHER
Edited by Joseph E. Maddy

I. ALBENIZ

PIANO CONDUCTOR

This Arrangement Copyright Edward B. Marks Music Corporation. Used by permission.

Figure 86

AMERICAN SALUTE

Based on "WHEN JOHNNY COMES MARCHING HOME"

Conductor

MORTON GOULD

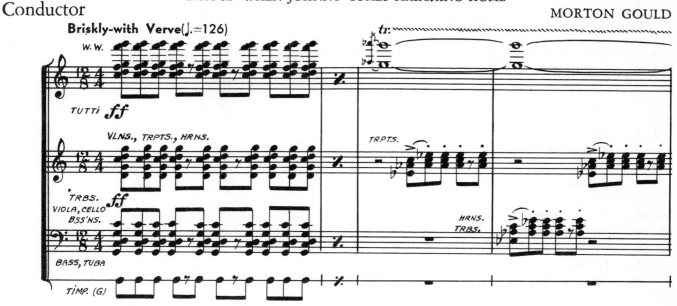

Figure 87

individual copies for each instrument from which every instrumentalist reads as he plays. Therefore, when ordering a composition from a music house or directly from the publisher ask for the score and parts. Specify the number of string parts needed by using numerals only. For example, one might order 8, 8, 6, 5, 4 which would be interpreted by the person filling your order to mean 8 first violin parts, 8 second violin parts, 6 viola parts, 5 cello parts and 4 bass viol parts.

The instruments on all scores appear in a definite order with very few exceptions. First, the wood-wind will be seen at the top of the page, next the brass instruments, then the percussion and last the strings. The harp, celesta and piano are used less often and are placed above the strings and below the percussion when included in the instrumentation. In a composition for solo instrument and orchestra as, for instance, the solo violin part in Mendelssohn's violin CONCERTO in E minor, the solo part is also found above the strings. It is also helpful to observe that the instruments of the wood-wind, brass and string families appear on the score in their respective groups in order of their pitch. The highest pitched instruments are at the top of each group. For example, in the wood-winds the piccolo is followed by the flutes, oboes, clarinets and bassoons. The one exception to this rule is found in the French horns which are placed directly under the wood-wind and above the trumpets. This is done because the horns are so often used with the wood-wind although they are, of course, brass instruments and belong in the brass family.

In Figure 88 we see the instrumentation used by Mozart in his SYMPHONY No. 40, in G minor. Figure 89 shows the orchestration employed by Strauss in the tone poem, DON JUAN. It will be seen that the basic family groups are the same in each case, the only difference being the much larger number of instruments found in the Strauss score. However, the standard instrumentation used by the great majority of composers lies between these two extremes and is as follows:

71

3	Flutes (the third player taking the piccolo part)
3	Oboes (the third player taking the English horn part)
3	Clarinets (third player taking the Bass clarinet part)
3	Bassoons (third player taking the Contra bassoon part)
4-5	French horns (the fifth player doubling the first part)
2-4	Trumpets
3	Trombones
1	Tuba
1-3	Percussion
1	Tympani
1-2	Harps
14-18	First violins
12-16	Second violins
10-12	Violas
8-10	Cellos
6-8	Bass viols

SYMPHONY No. 40
G Minor
Köch. No. 550

W. A. Mozart
1756-1791

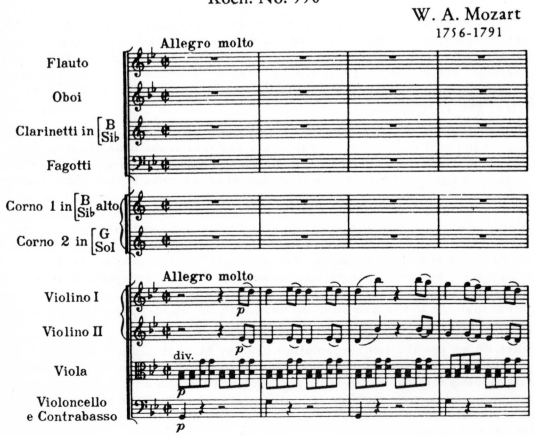

Figure 88

DON JUAN
op. 20

R. Strauss
1864—

Figure 89

SCORE MARKING

Score marking is a very individual matter for no two conductors use the same symbols nor will any two men mark exactly the same places throughout in a specific score. Some conductors are able to read a score with very few markings while others need a great many. There is at least one famous conductor who uses two scores. One he reserves for study purposes and this one he fills with pencilled indications of all descriptions while the other is marked sparingly for his use in public performance. There are a few general directions for the novice conductor to keep in mind as he approaches the problem of marking his first few scores after which he will have established his own pattern for placing pencilled indications on the score to assist him in actually conducting.

It is suggested that ordinary pencil be used in marking until enough experience has been gained to be certain that a mark on the score is the correct one and is there to stay. The student, before he has acquired this experience, can erase at will and gradually mark over the pencilled indications which he wishes to retain using a heavy colored pencil. Red or orange color will stand out most prominently on the page and should be used in preference to other colors. Do not mark with colored pencil scores which are rented or borrowed.

Cueing is one of the most important considerations in placing marks on a score. Study the composition in question, measure by measure, page by page, and mark all spots which, in your opinion, need to be cued. Use one of the following symbols: | 〔 〈 〈 or one of your own invention and place it at the exact spot where the entrance occurs. (Figure 90).

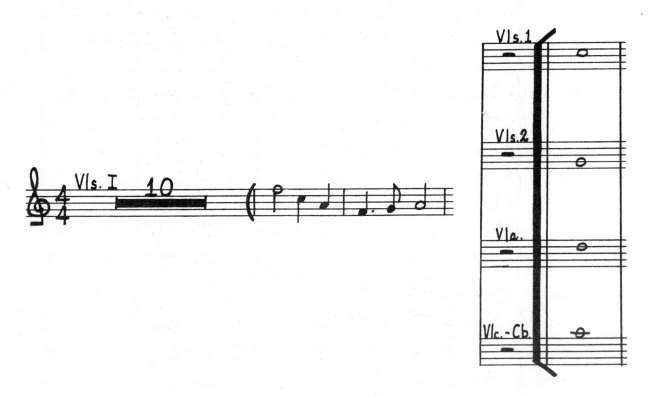

Figure 90

A cue is usually given to a player or players who have been resting for some measures and need to be reminded that it is time to play again. When there are two or more entrances at one time in fast tempos it may be impossible to indicate more than one entrance. In that case mark the one which is most important from a musical standpoint. Use the same symbol at all times so that it always has one meaning for you.

Melodic or rhythmic passages which the conductor wishes to emphasize may be marked by drawing a heavy jagged line under the passage as shown in Figure 91.

Figure 91

If a cue is needed for the entrance of one or more instruments <u>immediately</u> after a page turn it will help to write in the name of the instrument concerned in the right margin of the preceding page. This indication should always mean an <u>immediate</u> entrance of the instruments concerned--not an entrance which occurs several beats after the page is turned. This plan works equally well in cases where an important dynamic or tempo change occurs immediately after a page turn.

Sometimes the conductor needs to be certain that his attention will be shifted quickly from one extreme position on the score to another as, for example, from a flute solo to a cello section entrance. An arrow down the length of the score from the flute part to the cello part will serve very well in this instance. In extremely important places where the conductor must be especially alert draw a pair of eye glasses on the score to serve as a very special warning: ᴔ .

The circle ⓟ or square Ⓢ around dynamic markings serves to assist the eye. These symbols may be used around various words on the score such as mute, rall, accel., a2, a tempo and the like. If a score is a contemporary work there may be a section where the measure bar changes quickly from, for example, 4/4 to 6/8 to 2/4 to 5/4. Mark the measures where the changes occur with a large figure corresponding with the change in that bar. Such figures may be two or three inches high. In the same way very important dynamic changes may be written into the score when needed.

Remember that too many markings can be more confusing than helpful but bear in mind, too, that a mark on the score may be as helpful at times as a life preserver thrown to a man overboard. The finest conductors mark their scores and you need not be ashamed to do so. Above all do not go through the score you are studying underlining, circling and writing over in color all printed words and symbols, for you will find then that your markings are entirely too numerous to be helpful and that you have used colored pencil in dozens of places where you did not need such assistance. In other words, do not place a mark on your score without a very good reason.

SCORE READING

Reading well from a full score is a matter of much practice and experience. It is safe to say that few conductors can look at the page of a strange score and hear the notes printed upon it with their "inner" ear. That is, few conductors hear every note of the score as it would sound if an orchestra were playing it. The average student conductor probably will never attain such score reading proficiency. Score reading ability varies greatly with the individual just as the ability to sight read varies with instrumentalists. However, one's skill at reading a score can be improved by much practice.

It is wise to begin the practice of score reading by following a recording, score in hand, of one of the many string quartets available. After this the student is ready for a Haydn or Mozart symphony. He should then be prepared for the more complicated scores of the romantic and contemporary composers.

It is necessary to note on the margin of page one of your score the exact instrumentation, for all scores do not have the instruments listed in the margin of each page. It is also necessary to remember this listing, for even if the score selected for study should have every page so marked, there is no time when actually conducting to refer to them. Note, also, what keys are used for the transposing instruments. This check must be made at the beginning of each movement for the instrumentation may change from movement to movement.

Learn to use your score as a crutch but do not lean on it too heavily. Force yourself to look up often in conducting. Memorize sections of the score if you can. Above all, do not read the part of one instrument or one section only. For example, if you are a violinist do not keep your eyes glued to the violin part or the section of the score devoted to the strings. If you are a clarinet player do not watch the clarinet line or the wood-wind section only. Keep your eyes moving up and down the page at all times. Take in the general details of the score. Read ahead as much as possible for it is necessary that you anticipate such things as tempo changes, dynamic changes and cues. There is nothing worse than the conductor whose indications come after the orchestra has either passed the place in question or played the effect in spite of the conductor.

PRACTICING THE SCORE

You may purchase a piano reduction for study purposes. These are available for many standard orchestral works. A few of the many such piano reductions are:

SYMPHONY NO. 4 IN E MINOR by Brahms, published by Oliver Ditson Company.

SYMPHONY NO. 48 IN G MINOR by Mozart, published by Oliver Ditson Company.

THE NINE SYMPHONIES by Beethoven, for two hands, published by Edwin F. Kalmus.

SYMPHONY NO. 8 IN B MINOR by Schubert, (arranged by Moses) published by Carl Fischer.

SYMPHONY IN D MINOR (first movement) by Franck (arranged by Schmid) published by G. Schirmer.

Recordings are also an excellent aid in practicing your score. This means of study has its good and bad points, however. One advantage is that parts or sections of compositions may be repeated as often as desired. Also by this means the student is able to study the interpretations of the world's greatest conductors. The disadvantages lie in the fact that the student may tend to copy more than he should as well as fail to comprehend the tremendous difference between following a recording and being entirely responsible for all that happens when he is conducting.

Of course a live orchestra is the perfect medium for gaining experience after the score has been prepared carefully, but most students are not fortunate in having an orchestra available for this purpose.

Practice your score as you would a difficult instrumental composition. Work troublesome sections slowly, over and over again. Conduct in front of a mirror occasionally. In practicing your score you may have a pianist play it for you while you conduct if you are not able to hear it sufficiently well by simply reading the printed page. If you use this method insist that the pianist follow you exactly. One of the greatest difficulties the student encounters is that of coordinating what he sees on the score, what he hears and what he does with his body. Don't become absorbed in any one of these problems, forgetting the others. They must be one coordinated whole and equally stressed at least until the baton technique is automatic and the score reading reasonably fluent.

There are very few professional conductors who have the rare gift of a photographic memory. If you are so gifted then by all means memorize the complete score. However, do not attempt to conduct from memory unless you are able to recall every detail of the score. Beating time without a score is not conducting from memory. One must not rely on the musicians under direction for cueing or make mistakes of any kind, whether technical or musical. Keep the score in front of you at all times unless you have full confidence that you can do a perfect job in every respect without it.

CHAPTER XIII
Program Making

The care with which programs are selected for any orchestra regardless of technical proficiency can very well make the difference between the success and failure of any one concert or an entire season. Further, more than one conductor has failed to hold his post because of poor program building. The conductor must take into account the following factors (or those which apply to his situation) as he begins the task of planning a program:

Balance and Variety
Arrangement
Audience Appeal
Player Interest
Instrumentation
Timing

BALANCE AND VARIETY

Selecting a program for balance and variety is, in some respects, like planning a meal. The orchestra program must have balance and variety just as the well planned menu has. The most successful program will, therefore, contain music from more than one period as, for instance, the classic-romantic or romantic-contemporary schools or all three together. The latter in fact is the ideal program for the majority of audiences. It would be especially unwise to plan a program consisting of contemporary works exclusively for the average symphony audience is not at the present time willing to listen to an entire program of this type. By all means present contemporary music frequently on your programs. One does hear, occasionally, programs devoted entirely to one composer such as Wagner, Brahms, Tchaikovsky, Mozart or Beethoven but these one-composer programs are the exception rather than the rule.

Variety in music is as important as variety in daily life. Program content must vary in keys used, tempo, style and mood. Certainly no one would think of designing a program containing four slow movements from as many symphonies or eight overtures. Yet it is surprisingly easy to build programs which lack variety and which move too slowly. The conductor must beware of programming music which he himself especially prefers and forgetting the many considerations which must be weighed in good program building. There should be an attempt to open each program with a short and brilliant overture and to close with a piece for full orchestra which ends with a stirring climax.

ARRANGEMENT

Chronological order is not as vitally important as it once was. At least the conductor will not receive as much criticism if he mixes his program chronologically speaking, as he would have thirty years ago. Today one sees programs starting with a symphony, with overtures appearing in the middle of the program and with the classic work at the end while the concerto may appear anywhere at all. However, it can still be maintained that the preferred order is the chronological one when possible.

AUDIENCE APPEAL

The conductor through his orchestra is selling a product--music. If audience appeal is not taken into consideration the conductor's sales volume (ticket sales) will be more likely to go down than up. Each conductor will have his own particular problems in regard to this matter. It isn't necessary to play down to an audience in programming but neither should the director stubbornly decide that he is going to educate his listeners (and drive them away) by playing entire programs which they can't enjoy. It is much better to be wise and hold the audience by playing familiar compositions the second half of the concert or encores of a "pops" nature. It must be recognized that a "light" program in one situation may be a "heavy" one in another. The conductor must sense for himself what is best to program. Comments of listeners may be a guide as well as occasional questionnaires, providing the latter represent a majority response of the audience. There is no general rule for programming in respect to audience appeal except to try to satisfy every listener at least once during the concert. The conductor will invariably hear some critical comment after every program for, try as he will, he cannot satisfy every listener. Don't resent criticism. Instead, analyze it and if it is justified and can be used to strengthen your programming then adopt it.

Major symphonies while at home rarely gives encores. However, they usually do when they travel. The amateur and high school orchestras will find encores expected by the audience. Playing encores will give the conductor a chance to play light compositions thereby pleasing those in his audience who have not found anything on a particular program completely to their liking up to that point.

PLAYER INTEREST

This factor is not important in the case of professional orchestras but in amateur and school ensembles it is very important. When musicians are playing in an organization on a volunteer basis they like to have some choice in selection of material. Possibly they do not have the final decision as to program content but they must feel at times that they have had a voice in selection of music to be performed. This may take the form of expressing a preference for reading material or perhaps the forming of key players into a committee for program suggestion purposes. Some amateur and professional orchestras have program committees whose membership includes orchestra personnel and interested musicians in the community. Their responsibility is the gathering of program material from orchestras throughout the country and collaborating with the local conductor in building programs.

It is well to keep player interest by not selecting music which requires entire sections, such as the brass group, to sit with nothing to do for long periods of time. This applies especially to school and amateur orchestras. Music for school use should be chosen with the thought of keeping the second violin and viola parts as interesting to the player as possible.

Music chosen for amateur orchestras must be a challenge to the players but it must not be too difficult for the average ability of the group. In other words, the majority of the players must not lean on a few who can play their parts. Young players are retarded in their technical development when they have to consistently scramble for notes. This causes discouragement which in turn may result in the loss of players from an ensemble.

INSTRUMENTATION

The conductor must select music which fits his instrumentation. Every conductor will need to consider whether his program selections have in them solo passages which might prove too difficult for his first chair players. It is best for the director of an amateur or semi-professional orchestra to choose compositions for which there is a complete instrumentation available. In other words, it is better not to substitute instruments in this situation. In the professional orchestra players for instruments not commonly used can almost always be obtained on a temporary basis. The instrumentation will otherwise be complete in the professional ensemble. The school orchestra conductor may need to play arrangements of standard compositions which use substitutions for important parts and are liberally cross-cued. This is certainly permissible for sometimes in no other way can young players become acquainted with the standard orchestral literature. However, it is important to realize that a change of instrumentation destroys the original balance and color value the composer intended.

TIMING

The word timing, as used here, has to do with the total length of the program rather than the duration of individual numbers. A major symphony orchestra program lasts approximately an hour and three quarters, including an intermission of ten to fifteen minutes. This time length is rather long for amateur and school orchestra programs, for young players tire more quickly than professionals. Plan program length so that your audience leaves the hall stimulated by a short program rather than exhausted by a lengthy one. It is well to have an intermission when a program exceeds an hour. The intermission gives conductor, orchestra and audience a rest which makes possible a fresh playing and listening approach for the second half of the program. Study of the following well-planned programs will be helpful to the young conductor:

This is a program presented by the Lane Technical High School Orchestra of Chicago Illinois, P. W. Schneider, Director, and was the first half of a program shared with the Lane Concert Band, November 21, 1947.

Overture to Rosamunde. . . . . Schubert
Symphony in G Minor 1st Movement. . . . . Mozart
Suite from the Golden Cockerel . . . . Rimsky-Korsakow
Tarantelle from London Suite. . . . . Coates
Sword Dance from Gayne Ballet . . . . Khatchaturian

The Drake-Des Moines Symphony Orchestra, Des Moines, Iowa, Frank Noyes, Conductor, presented the following two programs on March 20, 1949 and March 11, 1951 respectively.

Overture to Egmont . . . . Beethoven
Concerto No. 4, D Major . . . . Mozart
     Joseph Fuchs, Violinist

Intermission

Introduction and Rondo Capriccioso . . . . Saint-Saens
Serenade to Music . . . . Williams
Porgy and Bess (A Symphonic Picture) . . . . . . Gershwin

Prelude, Choral and Fugue . . . . Bach-Abert
Concerto No. 2 in D minor . . . . Wieniawski
    Erica Morini, Violinist

Intermission

Symphony No. 1 in C minor . . . . Brahms

Concert given by the Iowa All-State Orchestra,

November 24, 1951, Frank Noyes, Conductor.

March from the "Suite Algerienne" . . . . Saent-Saens
Prelude, Choral and Fugue. . . . . Bach
Gweedore Brae . . . . Crowther
    (For Strings only)
Short Overture . . . . Gillis

This program was presented by the Cincinnati Symphony Orchestra, November 9, 1948, under the direction of Dr. Thor Johnson, at Des Moines, Iowa.

Overture, "Oberon" . . . . Carl Maria von Weber
Symphony No. 4 in F-minor, Opus 36 . . . . Peter Illyitch Tchaikovsky

Intermission

"The Portrait of a Frontier Town" . . . . Don Gillis
"The White Peacock" . . . . Charles Tomlison Griffes
Capriccio Espagnol, Opus 34 . . . . Nicolas Rimsky-Korsakov

CHAPTER XIV
Rehearsals

A book might easily be written on the subject of rehearsals. There is space in this discussion of the subject, however, for only a brief review of the more important factors the conductor must keep in mind during the rehearsal itself. Some important considerations in preparing for the first rehearsal are checking equipment, tryouts, marking music, readying the rehearsal room and other such duties. These details will not be discussed here. The professional conductor will have assistants for part of this work but the amateur and school conductor must at least supervise carefully all such preparations and in many instances do these tasks himself.

The rehearsal itself must start on time and must be thoroughly planned much as the football coach schedules his practices so that a specified period is devoted to each phase of the team's workout. For example, if the program consists of an overture, concerto and symphony the conductor must know which work he wishes to stress and what he plans to accomplish in the case of each composition.

The conductor is like a doctor, in the sense that the patient is the orchestra and he must diagnose its ailments, prescribe treatment and see that this treatment is properly applied. The most successful conductors are the ones whose keenness of hearing tells them what places in a composition need attention (diagnosis), whose inventiveness and background allow them to prescribe the proper remedies and whose personality, patience and leadership finally accomplish the task of correcting the weaknesses discovered. In other words, successful rehearsing really resolves itself into what the conductor hears and how cleverly he handles the corrective steps.

The first rehearsal is usually a reading one in the instance of the amateur and school orchestra. It may also be with the professional group if a new work is being rehearsed. The gradual refining process may take some time, in which case general corrections of mistakes must come before smaller and less obvious ones are worked out. A major mistake in a Boston Symphony Orchestra rehearsal might be the playing of one wrong note whereas an amateur orchestra might make so many errors of every kind the conductor would hardly know where to begin making order out of chaos. For this reason the conductor must know how much he can expect to accomplish in each rehearsal and how near perfection his group can finally play the music being programmed. Rehearsal order is an important consideration. Taking a short warm-up composition first with the most difficult work following while members of the group are fresh will result in greater accomplishment. Rest periods are also prescribed, for no instrumental organization can work at top efficiency for more than an hour at one time. A two hour rehearsal should certainly be broken into two sections by means of one intermission and it may be wise, in some instances, to divide such a practice into three periods by inserting two short rest periods.

Conductors in schools below college level must remember that in every rehearsal they are also instructors of every instrument in the orchestra. The orchestra is only as able as the individuals in it. Sectional practices are indispensable in the preparation of any orchestra and are best fitted into the rehearsal schedule after a general idea of a work has been had but before it has been practiced much.

At the rehearsal the conductor must listen for the following things:

(1) Intonation--Use a tuning bar or an electric tuning device and remember perfect tuning is no guarantee of perfect intonation. Players must listen to themselves

and to each other, adjusting their pitch to one another when necessary. Good listening means good pitch.

Just before the rehearsal begins allow a brief interval of time for checking, one at a time, the pitch of the strings, wood-wind and brass. Remember that the wood-wind and brass are affected by heat and cold and must warm up before testing their pitch. These instruments tend to change pitch during a rehearsal more than the strings and usually become sharp. Before going on the stage for a concert each individual instrumentalist should be checked for accuracy of tuning, a task which is usually performed by the section leaders concerned. Orchestras in this country use a variety of "A's" varying, generally, from 440 to 445 vibrations per second. It is essential that any instrumental organization settle on one definite pitch, preferably somewhere between 440 and 442. The 440 A may sound somewhat low or "flat" to some ears. However, the extreme high A's of 444 and 445 will cause definite problems in the brass and wood-wind sections. These instruments are not made to play that high with ease.

(2) Rhythm--Note values must be accurately read and rhythmic groups properly played. It is the conductor's job to hear such errors and right them. Some common rhythmic faults are the playing of triplets unevenly, lack of exactness among the strings in the values given three and four note chords and a tendency to shorten dotted eighth notes and lengthen sixteenth notes in combinations including these two. Lack of spacing (the period allowed between notes) in staccato and pizzicato passages is another common fault. This latter error causes a definite acceleration of the tempo. When

players fail to feel the rhythm in combinations such as $\frac{4}{4}$ ♩♩♩♩ it will help

them immeasurably if they will begin to count to themselves two to a bar to the conductor's four just preceding this rhythmic problem.

(3) Ensemble--Perfection of ensemble is one of the most important objectives of the director in rehearsing an instrumental group. Strict attention to the stick is the key in this vital matter and watching it must become automatic. The members of an ensemble can see if they will. They can be made conscious of the all-important matter of watching the baton carefully if the conductor will occasionally and without warning insert a sudden change of tempo, an accelerando or ritard, a hold or cut-off. This is especially true if he is having ensemble problems or feels that his group is inattentive. Such a device often injects some humor into the rehearsal and results in greater flexibility and control. Insist that each player sit so that he can see the baton easily. If the director's beat is clear and precise the ensemble should then be excellent.

(4) Balance--One of the conductor's jobs is the checking of the balance constantly at rehearsals. This is again a matter for the director to decide entirely for the player is in poor position to judge. In fact, during a final rehearsal the conductor may find it profitable to listen a few moments at the rear of the hall where the concert is to be held to check balance even more carefully.

The brass section of an orchestra will tend to play too loudly, particularly in classic works and in accompaniments. This is true of the percussion section, also, though conductors vary in regard to the amount of tonal volume they like to hear from this section. Wood-wind incidental solos are easily covered as are incidental solos by the principle string players. The string section, as a whole, will invariably play accompanying figures too heavily. Rehearse a passage part by part (melody, counterpoint, pure accompaniment) in order that the players may understand its construction. An understanding of the structure of a complicated section is always interesting to a group of instrumentalists and such analysis makes for better balance. Great care must be exercised if the accompaniments for guest soloists are to be kept in proper balance with the solo performer. When accompanying the conductor must be especially careful not to allow the orchestra to cover the soloist.

(5) Tone Quality--Instrumentalists very often play with a less beautiful tone than they are capable of producing either because of fatigue, carelessness or poor instrument adjustment. The conductor must be certain that his players are giving their best at all times. They need to be urged constantly to produce to the utmost of their capabilities. This is of particular importance in the string section. These musicians must constantly be checked and guided in use of vibrato and of the bow. Brass players must never be allowed to over blow. The percussion section needs careful coaching. For example, the cymbal can be exciting or just a noise. The tam-tam must be hit at an angle, otherwise its tone will sound strangled. The tone of the triangle can ring beautifully or be dull and lifeless.

(6) Phrasing--The score can convey in part only the artistry of phrasing inherent in the music. The conductor must be the players' advisor in all phrasing problems. What is done in this respect must be synchronized and coordinated until it is all a smoothly fitting part of the interpretive ideas of the conductor.

(7) Dynamics--Dynamics are the quantity of sound and its variance. An orchestra will disregard or play half-heartedly many dynamic markings unless constantly watched and checked. The final judge of how much forte here or piano there, how much crescendo or diminuendo must be the conductor's. A common fault of instrumental groups is the failure to return to the tonal level of the passage after making a crescendo followed by a diminuendo. This is especially true when these appear in series. The director must, by indicating them and through training and careful rehearsing, make the playing of dynamics, as written, a matter of habit.

(8) Technical Perfection--The rehearsal is, of course, the place to solve all technical problems. Sectional practice, slow practice, suggestions from the conductor for more simple ways of executing troublesome passages--all are part of the director's responsibility with technical help from section leaders available, if needed.

(9) General Interpretive Guidance--The conductor must be responsible for all questions of interpretation, must know what he wants and then see that his group gives him, as nearly as they are capable, just that. His guidance must result, for example, in Handel sounding like Handel and not Tchaikovsky or in Beethoven sounding as it should rather than Brahms in character. The conductor must be sensitive to the technical limitations of his players collectively and individually for he must not ask the impossible of them.

It is the duty of the conductor in rehearsal to inspire confidence among his players and a desire on the part of each one to give his best in beauty and variety of tone quality and technical accuracy. The final result will be sensitive, responsive playing so necessary to a truly finished and inspired performance.

Suggestions To The Conductor

Before the Rehearsal:

Place the order of the rehearsal on a blackboard.

Tune each section of the orchestra separately just before the rehearsal starts for better tuning results.

Learn all your scores before rehearsals.

Mark fingerings and bowings in the parts before rehearsal.

Make certain that rehearsal numbers or letters on your score are the same as those on the parts.

Arrange for the best possible lighting in the rehearsal room.

During the Rehearsal:

Project your voice so that every player can hear you.

Do not allow a forced tone quality from any individual or section.

Solo playing style is not orchestral playing style.

An orchestral pianissimo tone must have quality.

Do not neglect the percussion section.

Do not allow pizzicato passages to increase in tempo.

Choose words which will carry your exact meaning.

Lead your orchestra--do not let it lead you.

Check sections often for uniformity of bowing, fingering and breathing.

Teach your players to listen to each other as well as to themselves.

Spend more time rehearsing than talking.

Remember that your beat may be the cause of problems when they arise.

Focus your eyes carefully as you seek to transfer your messages to individuals and small groups while conducting.

Insist that every player sit so that he can see you easily.

Do not bluff where memory is concerned. Conduct from a score unless your memory is infallible.

Keep the rehearsal room at a comfortable temperature for better intonation and for maximum efficiency from your players.

Make players conscious of where the melody lies.

Do not neglect accompanying figures.

Check the type of bowings used by the strings and insist on uniformity in regard to the part, amount and speed of the bow employed.

Do not rehearse one group or section too long at a time in general rehearsals.

Deportment:

Save rehearsal time by training the members of your ensemble to stop playing immediately on signal.

Rap on the stand with the baton sparingly if at all.

Teach players to not give themselves away after making an error.

Remember that your audience listens with their eyes as well as with their ears.

When the violin and viola sections are at rest their instruments should assume a uniform appearance.

You and your players should applaud your soloist.

The inside player must turn the pages.

Do not allow your players to sit or stand in a slovenly way.

Morale:

Use humor occasionally to relieve tension and fatigue.

Take care of the manner in which you speak to an individual player.

When you make a mistake, admit it--don't blame the orchestra.

Begin rehearsals promptly and terminate them at the agreed time.

Be alert, sensitive, just; never impatient, sarcastic, indolent.

Do not be self critical thereby undermining yourself in the eyes of your organization.

BIBLIOGRAPHY

Baker: Dictionary of Musical Terms (New York, G. Schirmer Inc., 1895)

Berlioz: The Orchestral Conductor, Theory of His Art.(New York, Carl Fischer, 1902)

Bodegraven and Wilson: The School Music Conductor (Chicago, Hall & McCreary Co., 1942)

Braithwaite: The Conductor's Art (London, Williams and Norgate Ltd., 1952)

Burrows-Redmond: Symphony Themes (New York, Simon & Schuster, 1942)

Carse: Orchestral Conducting (London, Augener, 1935)

Earhart: The Eloquent Baton (New York, M. Witmark & Sons, 1931)

Finn: The Art of the Choral Conductor (Boston, C. C. Birchard and Company, 1939)

Finn: The Conductor Raises His Baton (New York and London, Harper & Brothers, 1944)

Finney: A History of Music (New York, Harcourt, Brace & Co., 1935)

Fuhr: Fundamentals of Choral Expression (Lincoln, University of Nebraska Press, 1944)

Gal: Directions for Score Reading (Austria, Wiener Philharmonischer Verlag, 1924)

Gehrkens: Essentials in Conducting (Boston, Oliver Ditson Co., 1919)

Goldman: The Band's Music (New York, Pitman Publishing Corporation, 1938)

Goldman: The Concert Band (New York and Toronto, Rinehart & Company, 1946)

Grove's: Dictionary of Music and Musicians (New York, The Macmillan Co., 1941)

Holmes: Conducting an Amateur Orchestra (Cambridge, Harvard University Press, 1951)

Krone: The Chorus and Its Conductor (Chicago, Neil A. Kjos Co., 1945)

Maddy and Giddings: Instrumental Technique for Orchestra and Band (Cincinnati, The Willis Company, 1926)

Norman: Instrumental Music in the Public Schools (Philadelphia, Oliver Ditson Company, 1941)

Prescott-Chidester: Getting Results with School Bands (New York-Boston-Chicago, Carl Fischer, Inc., and Paul A. Schmitt Music Company, Minneapolis, 1938)

Righter: Success in Teaching School Orchestras and Bands (Minneapolis, Paul A. Schmitt Music Company, 1945)

Scherchen: Handbook of Conducting (London, Oxford University Press, 1933)

Schmid: The Language of the Baton (New York, G. Schirmer Inc., 1937)

Schroeder: Handbook of Conducting (London, Augener Ltd., 1889)

Stoessel: The Technic of the Baton (New York, Carl Fischer, 1920)

Tandler: The Orchestral Manual (Los Angeles, Published by Author, 1946)

Van Hoesen: Handbook on Conducting (New York, F. S. Crofts & Co., Inc., 1944)

Weingartner: On Conducting (New York, E. F. Kalmus Scores, Inc., Original Edition 1895 in Germany)

Weingartner: On the Performance of Beethoven's Symphonies (London, Breitkopf & Hartel, 1908)

CHAPTER XV
The Concert Band

The modern concert band is a much younger organization than the symphony orchestra. The latter goes back for its beginning to the symphonic works of Haydn and Mozart while the symphonic band is a comparatively recent development. This fact is due mainly to the rapid improvement of the wind instruments over approximately the last half century plus the evolution during this period of a more standardized instrumentation. There is, even today, some variation in the concert band instrumentation as one compares such bands in the United States, France, Germany, England and Italy. In fact, European band libraries cannot readily be used by concert bands in this country. The repertoire for the concert band was for many years dependent in the main on arrangements taken from the symphonic and operatic literature so far as music by important composers was concerned. The standardization of the instrumentation and the improvement in the capabilities of the instruments have resulted in the availability of compositions by present day composers of international reputation such as Creston, Hindemith, Hanson, Copland and Milhaud, to mention a few. These composers and others have written works for the concert band in both small and large forms, including works of considerable magnitude.

The conductor of the concert band of today, therefore, must be equipped with a baton technique fully the equal of that of the orchestral conductor. There are no differences in this technical knowledge so far as the use of the baton is concerned. The fundamentals in a course in conducting are equally applicable whether the vehicle is ultimately the band or the orchestra. The band conductor must be a fine musician, be able to prepare his scores expertly, read them fluently and rehearse his organization efficiently. He must know clefs, transpositions and the limitations of the instruments under his direction. A working knowledge of the repertoire of the band must also be part of his equipment. It can readily be seen that much of this wealth of specialized knowledge cannot be included in a short course in baton technique but must be acquired in many courses in the music school curriculum such as basic and advanced instrumental methods, band technique and many other avenues of study not directly related to a course in conducting.

The seating arrangement of the concert band is not as standardized as that of the orchestra even though the latter has some variations. The following charts will give the young band conductor some ideas of the possibilities of band seating, though it will be necessary for him to use his own initiative in seating his own particular group in order to obtain the best possible musical and visual results.

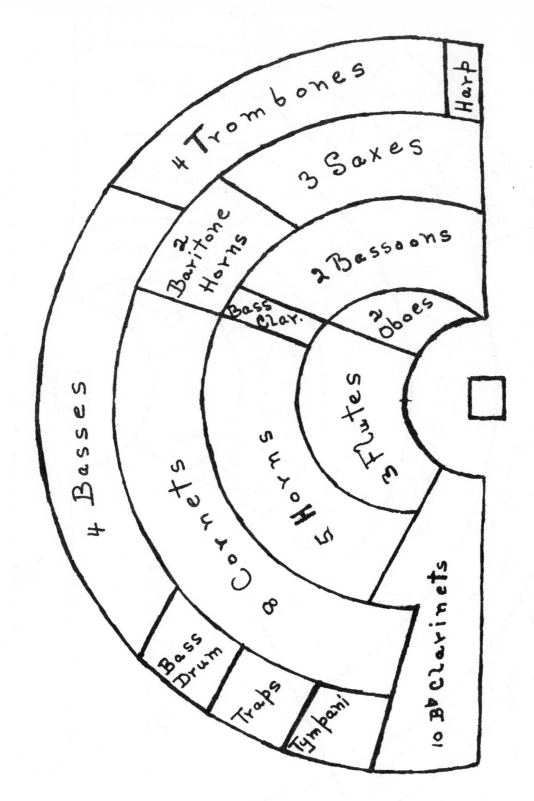

Figure 92. The United States Navy Tour Band, Commander Charles Brendler, Leader.

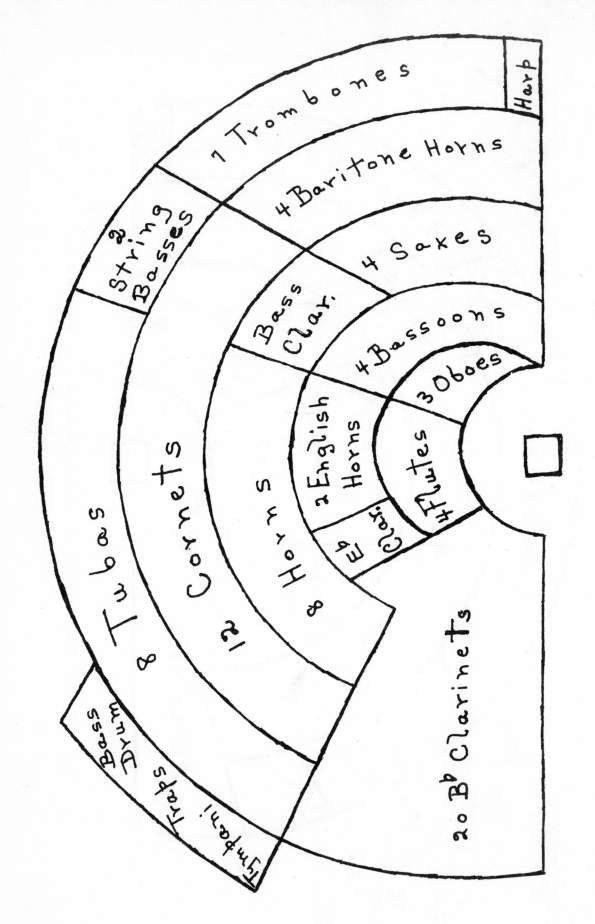

Figure 93. The United States Navy Full Band, Commander Charles Brendler, Leader.

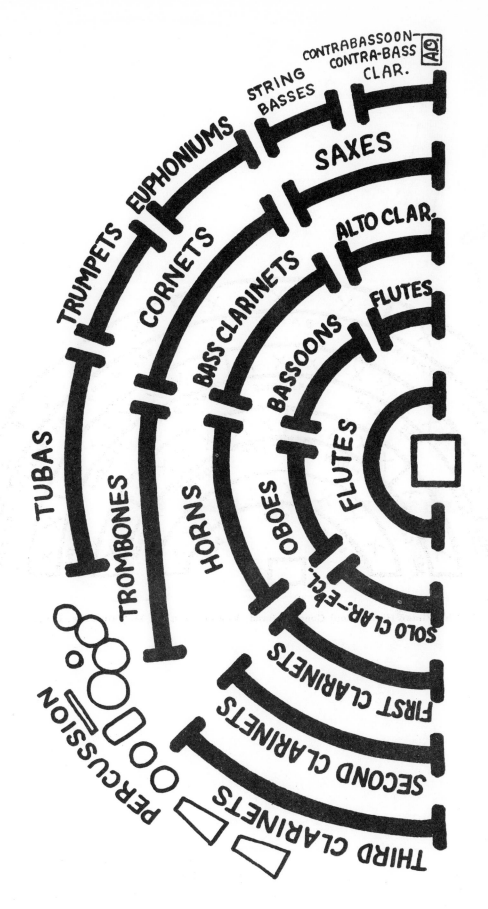

Figure 94. University of Michigan Symphony Band, Dr. William D. Revelli, Conductor.

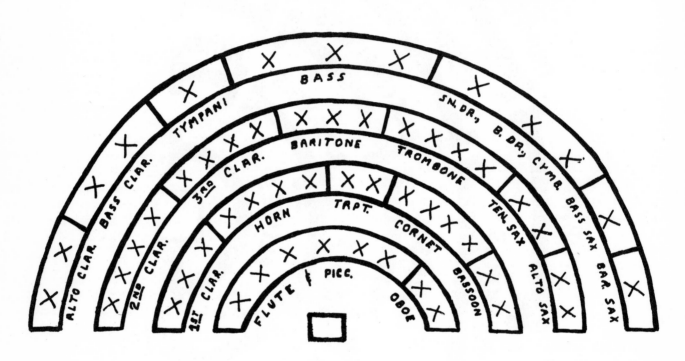

Figure 95. The Vinton High School Concert Band, Vinton, Iowa, T. M. Talmadge, Director.

CHAPTER XVI
The Chorus

The great majority of fine choral conductors employ conventional beat patterns and are as much at ease in directing instrumental ensembles as they are before their own groups so far as baton technique is concerned. There has been and probably will continue to be much discussion in regard to the question of whether the student looking toward choral specialization need have a separate course in order to acquire a desirable baton technique or whether he may obtain this fundamental technique in classes with instrumental students who are preparing for band and orchestral conducting.

The answer to the above question would seem to depend on the needs of the choral conductor as compared with those of the student in the other two fields of conducting endeavor. It is true that in choral conducting the indications for partial beats (syllables) must be given somewhat more frequently than in instrumental directing; however, these partial beats should not be indicated in a completely haphazard manner, as is so often done, nor more often than is necessary. When these partial beats occur they should be treated as subdivisions which they technically are, and should, therefore, follow the direction of the beat movement in which they are found. This technique is necessary not only for clarity and orderliness but also for the reason that choral groups should be trained to follow a conventional beat pattern, for many of the members of such ensembles may wish to sing at some time under a conductor whose technique of the baton follows the traditional patterns. Many choruses are trained for orchestral appearances by a choral expert before a final rehearsal or two under the conductor of the instrumental group with which the chorus is collaborating. This conductor will not vary his technique appreciably on arrival of the singers for his beat must also be a guide to the instrumentalists. That beat will invariably be a straight-forward, easy to read conventional one with the minimum of subdivisions and unnecessary flourishes.

There are many occasions when the choral director will wish to conduct instrumental groups, in which case he will save valuable rehearsal time, obtain better results and save himself embarrassment if his beat is easily read.

The argument that many singers are not trained musicians is not a valid reason for weak baton technique on the part of the director. Vocalists have fully as much talent and mental equipment as the average found in any group of musicians. Certainly it is no help to treat them as children or confuse them with unnecessary motions. In fact, they will become better musicians if they learn to rely upon themselves by being taught to read accurately, watch the baton and count carefully.

The conductor of a chorus in most instances deals with a smaller and more compact group than does the instrumental director. His ensemble has the added advantage of facing him directly. For that reason the use of the baton is often dispensed with though its use must still be considered a visual aid which is a very important argument for its use. In either case it must be remembered that his motions, unless the chorus is a very large one, need not be as broad as those of the conductor of large instrumental ensembles.

The arrangement of choral groups is fully as varied as those found in the previous study of the band and orchestra. The general musical and visual objectives are the same, however. Reasonable compactness is desirable which is best accomplished by employing three or four short rows rather than two longer ones. Traditionally, the upper voices are placed on the director's left and the lower voices on his right. The tenors and basses in mixed groups are sometimes placed in the center to give these singers added confidence as well as to obtain better intonation results. When possible, taller singers should be placed in the center of the group. In more recent years choral conductors have found that voices tune and blend better with outside voices together and inside voices likewise. Other directors use "mixed-up" seating.

When a piano is used, whether an upright or a grand, it should be located in front of and as near the center of the group as possible. The upright piano cannot be centered as can the grand for obvious reasons. In either case the pianist must be in a position to see every move of the conductor. Risers are a great assistance in projecting the voices and in adding to the general stage picture and should be used whenever possible.

As in the instance of the band and orchestral student conductors, no short course in baton technique can possibly include the very specialized learning necessary for choral conducting apart from the study of the technique of the baton. In addition courses in choral technique, private vocal lessons and many related courses are a necessity.

Figure 96 shows charts of the Drake University choir seating. This choir is conducted by Professor Stanford Hulshizer of the Fine Arts College faculty.

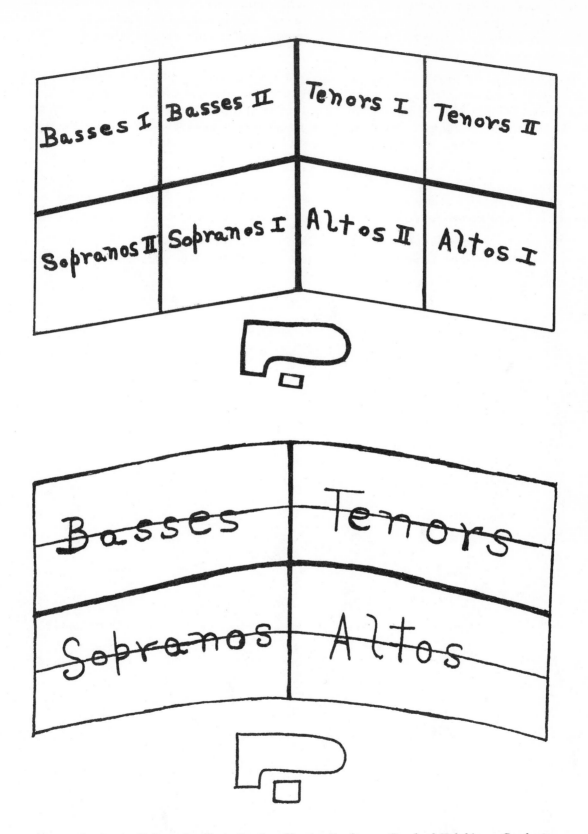

Figure 96. Drake University Choir Seating Charts, Professor Stanford Hulshizer, Conductor.